The William Greenberg

DESSERTS COOKBOOK

The William Greenberg DESSERTS COOKBOOK

CLASSIC DESSERTS FROM AN ICONIC NEW YORK CITY BAKERY

Carol Becker

Skyhorse Publishing

Skyhorse Publishing books may be purchased in bulk at special discounts for sales promotion, corporate gifts, fund-raising, or educational purposes. Special editions can also be created to specifications. For details, contact the Special Sales Department, Skyhorse Publishing, 307 West 36th Street, 11th Floor, New York, NY 10018 or info@skyhorsepublishing.com.

Skyhorse® and Skyhorse Publishing® are registered trademarks of Skyhorse Publishing, Inc.®, a Delaware corporation.

Visit our website at www.skyhorsepublishing.com.

10 9 8 7 6 5 4 3 2 1

Library of Congress Cataloging-in-Publication Data is available on file.

Cover design by Daniel Brount
Photographs by Laura Togut, except on pages 19 and 28 (courtesy of Getty Images).
Text by Sarah Jampel

Print ISBN: 978-1-5107-5179-8
Ebook ISBN: 978-1-5107-5180-4

Printed in China

For Emily and Alison

Contents

Introduction

It's no surprise that the New York City where I grew up is a far cry from the New York City where I live now. The small mom-and-pop shops, delis, and diners that used to be the epicenters of neighborhoods have been replaced by international chains that can afford the skyrocketing rents. While I still love this city I call home, it breaks my heart every time I see a long-standing favorite restaurant shutter or younger generations tire of running a family business in this tough environment.

Which is why when I was approached with the opportunity to buy William Greenberg Desserts in 2008, I jumped at the chance to preserve a part of the city I held so dear to my heart. I discovered the bakery when I moved into Manhattan from the Bronx at age 12 and it became a part of my family's life.

By the time I was an adult, running a fledging baking business as a second career, William Greenberg was an essential part of my routine—the place I'd go, even as a baker myself, to pick up delicious desserts for dinner parties and birthday celebrations. I knew that I wanted to do everything I could to keep it around and to honor the legacy Mr. Greenberg had worked so hard to foster while ushering it into a new era so that younger generations would be eager to support this local business.

Learning about the history of the bakery and the important role it played in the lives of so many families in New York made me very aware of the care and respect it merited. Much like this city's other institutions, like Russ & Daughters and Barney Greengrass, William Greenberg Desserts is woven into the fabric of the city. I love when customers come in and tell me stories of what the bakery means to them and share their memories about it.

But that success didn't come overnight. The bakery has been in business since 1946. As the legend goes, Mr. Greenberg acquired the funds to open shop during his journey home from World War II, where he served as a cook. He got so lucky playing cards—first on a transport train through liberated France and then on a ship crossing the Atlantic—that he returned to the city with enough money to fulfill his dream of opening a bakery.

He signed a lease on the Upper East Side of Manhattan and had the business savvy to include a clause that allowed him to vent the bakery's intoxicating aromas into the street. The smells of sweet cakes baking were irresistible to passers-by. And once potential customers walked through the door, they couldn't leave without at least a Black and White Cookie.

Because generations of New Yorkers have established memories around the taste of these treats, I've worked hard to maintain Mr. Greenberg's standard of excellence. We are committed to his ideals of using the best ingredients and impeccable techniques. Our Linzer Tarts (page 13) taste the same as they did more than six decades ago, as do all our long-standing treats.

Because the signature recipes are timeless and, frankly, delicious, they continue to sell at a rapid clip. Yet I also wanted to refresh the bakery and build memories for future generations who aren't nostalgic for the classics but who find excitement in discovering new sweet treats on their own. Without taking away Hamentaschen (page 27) or Rugelach (page 25), I added the Rainbow Cake (page 123) and Chocolate Snowflake Cookies (page 29). In some cases, I simply introduced old-fashioned desserts in new ways, like the red velvet or pumpkin versions of our classic Black and White Cookies.

Since Mr. Greenberg and I both began baking in home kitchens just like yours, you can be sure that the recipes in this book have been crafted with the amateur baker in mind. I may be the owner of a commercial bakery, but I am a home baker at heart. I learned to bake under the guidance of my Romanian grandmother Betty, who used to prepare all kinds of wonderful pastries and cookies in her tiny Washington Heights kitchen.

We rely on ingredients and equipment you likely already have, with the most advanced tool being a stand mixer like a KitchenAid. In most cases, you can even make do with handheld electric beaters, or, if you are really determined, arm strength and patience. You can assume that when a recipe calls for flour, unless specifically stated, we mean all-purpose, that when it calls for butter, we mean unsalted, and that when it calls for sugar, we mean granulated. Fancy ingredients are few and far between.

We have also worked hard to select a mix of easy baking recipes and more ambitious projects. Like the bakery, this book offers everything from daily little bites (try the Chocolate Chip Cookies on page 9) to weekend sweets (like the Raisin Scones, page 69) to special occasion and holiday desserts (like the very popular Strawberry Cream Cake, page 105). What makes William Greenberg Desserts unique is that all our treats are timeless. They are exactly the type of simple yet immensely satisfying sweets everyone wants all the time.

With this book, you have all the tools you need to make many of our desserts at home. My only hope is that whenever you're in the neighborhood, you'll still stop by to pick up a brownie and say hello.

The Cookie Box:

Cookies of All Shapes and Sizes

Black and White Cookies

Makes 10

I suspect many of you have opened this book for this recipe alone (but I do hope you find other treats that have piqued your interest too!). So yes, this is it—the iconic black and white cookie that William Greenberg Desserts is known for (and that Jerry Seinfeld brought to the national stage). Thanks to the combination of cake flour, buttermilk, and baking soda, our cookies are particularly soft and puffy and our signature icing is a shellac of fondant.

Cookies:

1¼ cups cake flour, sifted
½ teaspoon baking soda
½ teaspoon kosher salt
1 stick butter, softened
¾ cup sugar
1 egg
⅓ cup buttermilk
1 teaspoon vanilla extract

Icing:

3 cups confectioners' sugar
½ cup water
¼ cup light corn syrup
1 teaspoon cream of tartar
1 teaspoon vanilla extract
¼ cup semisweet chocolate chips

1. **Make the cookies:** Preheat oven to 350°F and line a baking sheet with parchment paper.
2. In a medium bowl, whisk together flour, baking soda, and salt.
3. In the bowl of a stand mixer fitted with a paddle attachment or working with electric beaters and a large bowl, beat butter and sugar on medium-high speed until light and creamy, 4 to 5 minutes.
4. Add egg and beat until just blended. Scrape down the sides of the bowl and add the buttermilk and vanilla, beating until smooth.
5. Reduce speed to low and gradually beat in the flour mixture just until no dry streaks remain.
6. Use a 2-ounce ice cream scoop to place scoops onto prepared baking sheet about 3 inches apart. Bake about 15 minutes, until golden and springy to the touch.
7. Cool on baking sheet for 5 minutes before transferring to a wire rack to cool completely.
8. **Make the icing:** In a double boiler or a medium heatproof bowl set over a pot of water, combine sugar, water, corn syrup, and cream of tartar. Bring the water in the pot to a soft boil over medium heat, then lower heat to a simmer and whisk the sugar mixture constantly until the mixture thickens, about 15 minutes. Remove from heat and stir in the vanilla. Divide between two bowls and add chocolate chips

to one bowl while fondant is still hot. Mix in the chips to combine, adding more hot water as needed to achieve a spreadable consistency.

9. Spread vanilla icing on half of the flat side of each cookie, then frost the other halves with chocolate icing. Add hot water to the bowls of icing by the ½ teaspoon to maintain a spreadable consistency. Let set for 30 minutes before serving.

Do-ahead: *Cookies can be made 4 days ahead. Store in an airtight container in the refrigerator.*

Passover Black and White Cookies

Makes about 16 large cookies

Our customers love our Black and White Cookies so much they can't go without them during Passover when they give up flour. To help satisfy their cookie cravings, we make a Passover version using a combination of potato starch and matzoh cake meal. Compared to the original, the base has a cakier texture, but the frostings taste the same.

Note: Matzoh cake meal is finer than regular matzoh meal. Be sure to seek it out for a fine-textured cookie.

Cookies:

1¾ cups potato starch
¾ cup matzoh cake meal
1 teaspoon baking powder
½ teaspoon kosher salt
½ cup margarine, softened
1 cup granulated sugar
4 large eggs
2 teaspoons vanilla extract
1 tablespoon fresh lemon juice
⅓ cup unsweetened almond milk

Icing:

⅔ cup granulated sugar
1½ cups confectioners' sugar*
½ teaspoon fresh lemon juice
½ teaspoon vanilla extract
3½ ounces semisweet chocolate, chopped

*To make Passover confectioners' sugar, pulse 1½ cups granulated sugar and 2 tablespoons potato starch together in a food processor.

1. **Make the cookies:** Preheat the oven to 325°F. Line 2 cookie sheets with parchment paper.
2. In a small bowl, whisk the potato starch, matzoh meal, baking powder, and salt.
3. In a stand mixer fitted with the paddle attachment or working with electric beaters and a large bowl, beat the margarine and granulated sugar together on medium until creamy. Add the eggs, vanilla, and lemon juice and beat until well combined, 2 to 3 minutes; the mixture will look curdled. Stir in the almond milk. Reduce speed to low and gradually add the dry ingredients until fully incorporated.
4. Drop the batter using a 2-ounce cookie scoop (or ¼ cup measuring cup) 2 inches apart onto the prepared sheets. Bake, one sheet at a time, until the tops are dry and spring back to the touch when lightly pressed, about 15 minutes. Cool completely on the sheets on wire racks.
5. **Make the icings:** In a small saucepan, combine the granulated sugar and ½ cup water. Bring to a boil, stirring to dissolve the sugar. Remove from the heat and cool to room temperature.
6. Put the confectioners' sugar in a medium bowl. Bring 2 tablespoons water to a boil in a saucepan or microwave and add to the bowl, along with the lemon juice and vanilla. Stir until smooth. The white icing should be a

spreadable consistency, neither runny nor stiff. If the icing is too stiff, stir in the sugar syrup, a tablespoon at a time, until soft enough to spread.

7. Melt the chocolate in a heatproof bowl set over a saucepan of simmering water or in 20-second increments in the microwave. Stir until smooth then allow to cool slightly. Add the sugar syrup, a tablespoon at a time, until the chocolate is soft enough to spread; it will initially firm up, but loosen again with additional syrup. Spread the flat sides of the cookies with white icing on one half and black on the other half. Let stand on a rack until the icings set.

Do-ahead: *The cookies can be made 5 days ahead. Store in an airtight container.*

Black and White and Frosted All Over

I know it's not nice to play favorites, but I must make a confession: if there's one chosen child at William Greenberg—one dessert that the bakery is known for more than anything else—it's the Black and White Cookie. Mr. Greenberg did not invent the black and white—its exact origins are fuzzy, but is thought to have made its debut in upstate New York—he did perfect it.

While you might be able to find one in nearly every bodega, deli, diner, and corner store in New York City, our version is unparalleled in taste and texture. It's more similar to a personal-sized cake than a cookie, with a soft, puffed base covered in equal parts chocolate and vanilla frosting.

I've taken the responsibility of continuing Mr. Greenberg's legacy of excellent Black and White Cookies very seriously. We still churn out the classic black and whites but also create custom colors for weddings, graduations, sports events, baby showers, bar mitzvahs, reunions, camp, and every holiday. We send cookies home with our regulars and locals, but also with tourists who have traveled far and wide for the sole purpose of buying boxes as souvenirs. And now we ship all over the world.

Even though I grew up eating William Greenberg's black and whites and am now in charge of overseeing the thousands we sell weekly, both in store and online, I'm not sick of them. Not even close. I still have fun dreaming up new ways to play with the cookie. My favorite versions might be the ones we sell from October to the end of the year which we make fall-appropriate by adding pumpkin or sweet potato to the cookie base. I hope you can take the recipe (page 2), make it as William Greenberg intended, and then take a turn making it your own too!

Chocolate Chip Cookies

Makes 5½ dozen

Our chocolate chip cookies, which have been at the store since the beginning, aren't the gargantuan behemoths you see at lots of bakeries nowadays—instead, they're crispy, crunchy, and delicate. At the bakery we sell the bite-sized cookie by the pound, which means customers can polish off a good amount on their walk home and their families will never know a thing. If I'm ever faced with too many, I like to crumble them up and fold them into softened ice cream or grind them in the food processor, mix with melted butter, and use as the base for a press-in tart.

3 sticks butter, softened
1 cup light brown sugar
1 egg
½ teaspoon vanilla extract
1½ cups flour
¼ teaspoon kosher salt
2 cups chocolate chips, divided

1. Preheat oven to 325°F. Line two baking sheets with parchment paper.
2. In the bowl of a stand mixer or working with electric beaters in a large bowl, cream together butter and sugar on medium-high speed until light and fluffy, 4 to 5 minutes, scraping the bowl occasionally.
3. Add egg and vanilla and beat to combine. Add flour and salt and pulse mixer to incorporate. Mix on low just until no dry spots remain. Stir in 1 cup chocolate chips.
4. Drop dough by rounded teaspoonfuls onto prepared baking sheets. Bake 10 to 12 minutes, until set and golden.
5. Cool on baking sheets for a few minutes, then transfer to a wire rack to cool completely.
6. To optionally dip the cookies in chocolate, melt the remaining cup of chocolate in a double boiler or in the microwave in 20-second increments, then dip each cookie to half-cover them in chocolate.

Do-ahead: *Cookies can be stored in an airtight container for 3 to 4 days.*

Big Sprinkle Cookies

Makes 18 cookies

When I acquired the bakery in 2008, it had been in business for more than sixty years. Suddenly, I had the chance to add my own recipes to the menu—but I didn't want to add just anything. I needed to make sure every new menu item fit seamlessly with the old-school vibe. These soft, colorful cookies came to mind immediately and became my first addition.

2½ cups flour
1 teaspoon baking powder
¼ teaspoon baking soda
½ teaspoon kosher salt
2 sticks butter, softened
¼ cup cream cheese, softened
1½ cups sugar
1 egg
2 teaspoons vanilla extract
½ teaspoon almond extract
1¾ cups rainbow sprinkles

1. In a medium bowl, whisk together flour, baking powder, baking soda, and salt.
2. In the bowl of a stand mixer fitted with a paddle attachment or working with electric beaters and a large bowl, cream butter, cream cheese, and sugar together on medium-high speed until light and fluffy, 4 to 5 minutes, scraping down the sides of the bowl twice during mixing.
3. Add egg, vanilla extract, and almond extract, and mix to combine.
4. Reduce speed to low and add the flour mixture, mixing just until no dry spots remain. Scrape the dough out onto a sheet of plastic wrap, shape into a disc, wrap, and chill for at least 1 hour.
5. Preheat oven to 350°F and line two baking sheets with parchment paper. Roll 2 heaping tablespoons of dough into balls. Roll balls in rainbow sprinkles, covering each completely.
6. Place about 4 inches apart on the lined baking sheets, then flatten to ½-inch thick with the bottom of a glass.
7. Bake 16 to 18 minutes, or until set and slightly golden around the edges. Let cool slightly on the baking sheet, then transfer to a wire rack to cool completely.

Do-ahead: *Cookies can be made 5 days ahead. Store in an airtight container at room temperature.*

Do-ahead: *Cookies can be made 4 to 5 days ahead. Store unfilled in an airtight container at room temperature and fill the day of serving.*

Linzer Tarts

Makes 18 to 24 sandwiches

These coaster-sized linzers—crumbly, melt in your mouth shortbread sandwiched with raspberry jam—are a staple at the bakery. But that doesn't mean you can't change them up to your liking. Substitute in another type of nut flour, like almond or pecan or even pistachio for the hazelnut flour. Switch the spice from cinnamon to cardamom. Use blueberry or apricot jam in place of raspberry. Or coat half of the assembled sandwich in melted chocolate. You can also use a smaller round cutter—just keep a close eye as they're baking, as a smaller cookie will brown more quickly.

6 cups flour
1½ cups hazelnut flour
1 tablespoon cinnamon
1 tablespoon baking powder
1 teaspoon kosher salt
3 eggs
½ teaspoon vanilla extract
6 sticks butter, softened
2 cups sugar
Raspberry preserves

1. In a large bowl, whisk together the flour, hazelnut flour, cinnamon, baking powder, and salt. In a small bowl, whisk together the eggs and vanilla.
2. In the bowl of a stand mixer fitted with a paddle attachment or working with electric beaters and a large bowl, cream together butter and sugar on medium speed until light and fluffy, 4 to 5 minutes, scraping down the sides of the bowl occasionally.
3. Reduce the speed to low and add the flour mixture in thirds, alternating with the egg mixture in two additions, until you have a soft dough.
4. Turn the dough out onto a sheet of plastic wrap and divide in 4. Shape each into a disc, wrap in plastic, and chill for at least 4 hours and up to 1 day.
5. Preheat oven to 325°F and line two baking sheets with parchment paper.
6. Working with one disc at a time, roll out dough to ¼-inch thick on a lightly floured surface. Use a 3½-inch round or fluted cookie cutter to cut cookies, then use a smaller cutter to cut the centers out of half of the cookies. (You can gather the first round of scraps, form into discs, refrigerate until firm, and reroll once.)
7. Place the cookies 2 inches apart on prepared baking sheets and bake for 20 to 25 minutes, or until lightly golden.
8. Allow cookies to cool slightly on the baking sheets, then transfer to wire racks to cool completely. Once cool, spread the preserves on the bottom halves. Gently place on the cookie tops.

Raspberry Thumbprint Cookies

Makes 5½ dozen cookies

A tender, buttery cookie with a jammy center, these thumbprints are a favorite with children and adults alike. The moldable dough holds it shape in the oven, acting as a barrier for the jammy center. Use any kind of jam you like or try filling each one with a chocolate kiss or a spoonful of homemade frangipane.

2 cups flour
½ teaspoon baking powder
¼ teaspoon kosher salt
2 sticks butter, softened
¾ cup sugar
2 egg yolks
1¼ teaspoons vanilla extract
¼ teaspoon almond extract
Raspberry preserves

1. In a small bowl, whisk together the flour, baking powder, and salt.
2. Working with a stand mixer fitted with a paddle attachment or with electric beaters and a large bowl, cream together the butter and sugar on medium speed until light and fluffy, 4 to 5 minutes. Add the egg yolks one a time, beating to incorporate after each addition and scraping down the sides of the bowl as necessary. Mix in the vanilla and almond extract. Reduce the speed to low and add the flour mixture. Pulse until no dry spots remain.
3. Turn the dough out onto a sheet of plastic wrap, shape into a disc, wrap, and chill for at least 1 hour.
4. Preheat the oven to 325°F and line two baking sheets with parchment paper. Roll heaping teaspoonfuls of dough into balls and place 2 inches apart on prepared baking sheets. With your thumb, make an indent in the center of each cookie and fill with about ½ teaspoon jam.
5. Bake 10 to 12 minutes, until golden and set. Cool slightly on baking sheets before transferring to wire racks to cool completely.

Do-ahead: *Cookies can be made 1 week ahead. Store in an airtight container at room temperature. Dough can be made 24 hours ahead. Let soften slightly at room temperature before shaping into balls.*

Do-ahead: *Dough logs can be made 24 hours ahead and kept refrigerated. Cookies can be made 5 to 6 days in advance. Store in an airtight container.*

Pecan Sandies

Makes 5 dozen

Like our Chocolate Chip Cookies (page 9), these tender and crumbly token-sized shortbread are sold by the pound—it's just that easy to go through a whole bunch in one sitting. Don't worry about making the logs perfectly round and consistent in diameter; even I struggle with that part, and they still come out delicious every time.

2½ sticks cups, softened
7 tablespoons sugar, divided
½ cup (1½ ounces) ground pecans
¼ teaspoon kosher salt
2 egg yolks
¼ teaspoon vanilla extract
1¾ cups flour

1. In the bowl of a stand mixer fitted with a paddle attachment or working with electric beaters and a large bowl, cream the butter, 6 tablespoons sugar, pecans, and salt on medium speed until light and fluffy, 4 to 5 minutes. Add the egg yolks one at a time, beating well to incorporate after each addition and scraping down the sides of the bowl as necessary. Beat in the vanilla.
2. Reduce speed to low and gradually add the flour, beating until no dry streaks remain.
3. Transfer half the dough onto a sheet of lightly floured parchment paper. With floured hands, gently pat the dough into a fat cylinder shape. Use the floured parchment to help you roll each half into a log that is 1 inch in diameter and about 15 inches long, adding more flour as necessary to prevent sticking. Repeat with the other half of the dough, forming 2 logs total.
4. Cover with plastic wrap and transfer to the fridge for at least 1 hour, until the dough is very firm.
5. Preheat oven to 325°F. Line two baking sheets with parchment paper.
6. Slice into ½-inch discs, then place 1 inch apart on the prepared baking sheets.
7. Bake 20 to 25 minutes, or until set and golden brown.
8. Allow to cool for 5 minutes on baking sheets, then sprinkle with remaining 1 tablespoon sugar and transfer to wire racks to cool completely.

Cinnamon Sugar Butter Horns

Makes about 24

One of my sweetest memories of childhood is visiting my grandmother in Washington Heights. She made these yeasted crescent-shaped cookies stuffed with walnut cinnamon-sugar that were like rugelach but softer and airier. I'd eat them warm, right off the baking sheet. This is her famous recipe—and the cookie that made me want to start baking. They may be a bit more involved than the others in this book—you have to wait for the dough to rise and shape each one—but they are so worth it!

- ¼ cup warm water (between 100 and 110°F)
- 1½ cups plus 1 teaspoon sugar, divided
- 2 envelopes (4½ teaspoons/ 14 grams) active dry yeast
- 4½ cups flour, divided
- 2 eggs
- 1 stick butter, melted and cooled, plus 2½ sticks, very soft
- ½ cup warm milk (between 100 and 110°F)
- 2 tablespoons sour cream
- 1 teaspoon kosher salt
- 2 tablespoons cinnamon
- 2 cups (8 ounces) finely chopped walnuts

1. In a small bowl, combine the water and 1 teaspoon of sugar. Stir in the yeast and let sit 5 to 10 minutes, until mixture is foamy. (If your mixture doesn't foam, your yeast may be dead—get new yeast and try again.)
2. In a medium bowl, stir together 3¾ cups of flour, ½ cup sugar, eggs, the ¼ pound melted butter, milk, sour cream, salt, and the yeast mixture, and mix well. Cover and refrigerate 1 hour.
3. In a medium bowl, use a wooden spoon or sturdy plastic spatula to thoroughly mix 2 sticks (½ pound) very soft butter and remaining ½ cup flour until no dry spots remain. On a generously floured surface, roll out refrigerated dough into a 12 x 18-inch rectangle. Use a spatula to spread butter mixture over refrigerated dough. Roll into a log until you can no longer see the butter, then pat into a flat rectangle about 1 inch thick, wrap with plastic wrap, and refrigerate overnight or at least 8 hours.
4. Preheat oven to 375°F. Line two baking sheets with parchment paper.
5. In a medium bowl, mix cinnamon and remaining 1 cup sugar. Transfer dough to a lightly floured surface and divide in two. Keep one half refrigerated while you roll the other half into a circle about 13 inches in diameter and a scant ¼-inch thick. Gently spread 2 tablespoons of the remaining very soft butter over the dough, then sprinkle with half of

the cinnamon-sugar. Top with half of the walnuts in an even layer, pressing gently so that it all adheres. Using a pizza cutter or a very sharp knife, cut the circle into 12 even triangular slices. Starting at the wide end, tightly roll each slice toward the center of the circle. Place 2 inches apart on prepared baking sheets with the point underneath and curve the ends slightly toward the center to form a crescent. Repeat with the remaining dough and filling.

6. Bake for 20 to 25 minutes until firm and golden. Let cool for 10 minutes on baking sheet, then transfer to wire racks to cool completely.

Do-ahead: *Cookies can be made 3 to 4 days ahead. Store in an airtight container.*

Do-ahead: *The biscotti can be made up to 1 week ahead. Store in an airtight container.*

Chocolate Pistachio Biscotti

Makes about 2 dozen

One of my daughters thinks chocolate is a food group. That inspired me to create these cookies, which are different from the usual pale nut-based biscotti. Even though I don't like chocolate much, I love these. They're softer than the standard biscotti with a fudgy middle. The top sparkles with sugar, which also helps balance the chocolate's bitterness. If you prefer crunchy biscotti, bake the slices for an additional five minutes.

1 stick unsalted butter
4 ounces semisweet chocolate, chopped
1¾ cups all-purpose flour
½ cup Dutch-processed unsweetened cocoa powder
1½ teaspoons baking powder
½ teaspoon kosher salt
2 large eggs
1 cup sugar, plus more for sprinkling
1 teaspoon pure vanilla extract
1 cup shelled unsalted pistachios

1. Preheat the oven to 350°F. Line a large baking sheet with parchment paper.
2. In a heatproof bowl set over a saucepan of simmering water or in the microwave in 20-second increments, melt the butter and chocolate together, stirring until smooth. Remove from the heat.
3. In a large bowl, sift together the flour, cocoa, baking powder, and salt.
4. In a stand mixer fitted with a paddle attachment or working with electric beaters and a large bowl, beat the eggs and sugar on medium speed until aerated and pale, about 2 minutes. Add the vanilla. Beat in the chocolate mixture until smooth. Reduce speed to low and stir in the flour mixture until just blended. Fold in the nuts. The dough will be sticky.
5. On the prepared baking sheet, form the dough into one log 10 inches long, 1½ inches tall, and 3½-inch-wide. Sprinkle log with sugar.
6. Bake for 25 minutes. Transfer the baking sheet to a cooling rack. Reduce the oven temperature to 275°F.
7. When the log is cool enough to handle, carefully transfer to a cutting board and use a serrated knife or sharp chef's knife to cut it into ½-inch slices, then return to the baking sheet in a single layer, cut sides up. Bake for 10 to 15 minutes more, until cookies are crisp.
8. Cool completely on a wire rack.

Cranberry Almond Biscotti

Makes about 20

These easy stir-by-hand biscotti showcase the unique tanginess of cranberries. Plumped in hot water, the dried berries stay tender in the crunchy almond cookie. I even use their soaking liquid to impart more tart fruit flavor in the dough, which is scented with orange, cinnamon, and vanilla, too.

- 1 cup dried cranberries
- 2 large eggs
- ¾ cup sugar, plus more for sprinkling
- ½ cup vegetable oil
- 1¼ teaspoons baking powder
- 1 teaspoon ground cinnamon
- 1 teaspoon pure vanilla extract
- ½ teaspoon pure almond extract
- ½ teaspoon pure orange extract
- ¼ teaspoon kosher salt
- 2½ cups flour, plus more as needed
- 1 cup slivered almonds

1. Preheat the oven to 350°F. Line a large baking sheet with parchment paper.
2. Place the cranberries in a small bowl and cover with hot water. Let stand for a few minutes to soften. Drain, reserving the liquid.
3. In a large bowl, whisk the eggs, sugar, vegetable oil, baking powder, cinnamon, vanilla, almond extract, orange extract, and salt until smooth. Add the flour, almonds, cranberries, and 2 tablespoons cranberry liquid. Stir until all the flour is incorporated and a sticky dough forms.
4. Scrape the dough onto the prepared baking sheet. With slightly damp hands, form the dough into a log 10 inches long, 1½ inches tall, and 4 inches wide. Sprinkle the log with sugar.
5. Bake for 25 minutes. Transfer the baking sheet to a cooling rack.
6. When the log is cool enough to handle, cut it into ½-inch slices and return to the baking sheet in a single layer. Bake for 20 minutes more, until lightly golden and dry throughout.
7. Cool completely on a wire rack.

Do-ahead: *The biscotti can be made up to 1 week ahead. Store in an airtight container.*

Do-ahead: *The rugelach can be made 3 days ahead. Store in an airtight container at room temperature.*

Rugelach

Makes 4 dozen

Mr. Greenberg's aunt passed down the recipe for this very traditional Eastern European rolled cookie. The pastry is very flaky and buttery and tastes delicious with a wide variety of fillings. The raspberry jam variation below is one of the most popular at our bakery and the easiest option, but you can also use melted chocolate, cinnamon-sugar, ground walnuts mixed with spice and sugar, dried apple filling, or any other fruit jam. After much experimentation, I've found that the best method for the pastry is to mix all the ingredients together in a food processor. That and practice. The more rugelach you make, the flakier they'll be. Once you get a feel for the dough, you can handle it very gently to ensure the most tender pastry.

- 8 ounces cream cheese, cut up, softened
- 2 sticks unsalted butter, cut up, softened
- 2 cups flour, plus more for dusting
- 2 tablespoons sugar
- ½ teaspoon kosher salt
- 1 cup raspberry jam

1. In a food processor, combine the cream cheese, butter, flour, sugar, and salt. Pulse, scraping the bowl occasionally, until there are no streaks of flour and the dough forms loose, large clumps. Turn the clumps out onto a lightly floured work surface and divide into four equal piles with lightly floured hands. If you have a kitchen scale, use it to measure the total weight, then divide by four to divvy up the dough perfectly.
2. Gently gather one pile of dough into a disc on a sheet of wax paper. Top with another sheet of wax paper and gently roll into a ¼-inch-thick round, about 6 inches in diameter. Repeat with the remaining dough. Refrigerate the rounds until firm, at least one hour.
3. Preheat the oven to 350°F. Line cookie sheets with parchment paper. If the dough has firmed up too much to bend without cracking, let it sit at room temperature until pliable.
4. Remove the top sheet of wax paper from 1 dough round. Spread evenly with one quarter of the jam. Cut the round into 12 even wedges like a pizza. Roll one wedge up from the wide end to the tip and transfer to a prepared sheet with the tip tucked underneath against the pan. Repeat with the remaining wedges, spacing them 1 inch apart. Chill cookies for 30 minutes before baking.
5. Bake one sheet at a time until golden and baked through, 18 to 20 minutes. Cool completely on the sheets on racks. Repeat with the remaining rounds and jam.

Hamentaschen

Makes 4 dozen

Come Purim, which usually falls between February and March, our bakery displays are crammed full of all varieties of these triangle-shaped cookies. All the classics—apricot, cherry, prune, and poppy—alongside some newfangled versions like chocolate, halvah, and marzipan. It's fun to shape the cookies, especially with kids, but the dough can be soft and sticky. Be sure to work quickly and keep the dough as cool as possible.

4 sticks butter, softened
1¼ cups sugar
5 egg yolks
½ teaspoon vanilla extract
4½ cups flour
½ teaspoon kosher salt
Smooth raspberry or apricot preserves

1. In the bowl of a stand mixer fitted with a paddle attachment or using electric beaters and a large bowl, cream together the butter and sugar on medium speed until light and fluffy, 4 to 5 minutes.
2. Reduce speed to low and add the egg yolks, one by one, beating to combine after each addition and scraping down the sides of the bowl as necessary. Add the vanilla and mix to combine. Add the flour and salt and pulse until no dry spots remain and a soft dough forms. Shape into a disc and refrigerate, covered, for at least two hours.
3. Preheat the oven to 325°F and line two baking sheets with parchment paper.
4. Divide dough in half and keep one half wrapped in plastic and refrigerated. On a lightly floured surface, roll out chilled dough to ¼-inch thick. Cut into 2½-inch circles using a cookie cutter or glass cup and transfer to prepared sheet.
5. Dollop the middle of each dough round with 1 teaspoon of preserves.
6. Fold up three sides so that the round becomes a triangle and pinch the corners to seal them. Bake 15 to 18 minutes, until golden and firm. Cool for 5 minutes on baking sheets, then transfer to cooling racks to cool completely.
7. Repeat with remaining dough.

Do-ahead: *Dough can be made one day ahead. Cookies can be made 2 to 3 days ahead. Store in an airtight container.*

Chocolate Snowflake Cookies

Makes 3 dozen

When I was trying to think of a festive, wintry dessert to add to our roster, I remembered the batches of dense, gooey-in-the-middle chocolate cookies I often received as presents during the holiday season. As the balls of dough, which are rolled in confectioners' sugar before they are baked, spread in the oven, the sugar separates, creating all sorts of intricate striations and designs. Every cookie is different but beautiful, just like a snowflake.

2 cups sugar
½ cup vegetable oil
4 ounces unsweetened baking chocolate, melted
4 eggs
2 teaspoons vanilla extract
2 cups flour
2 teaspoons baking powder
½ teaspoon kosher salt
¾ cup confectioners' sugar, sifted

1. In the bowl of a stand mixer or working with a handheld electric mixer and large bowl, combine sugar, oil, and melted chocolate and beat on medium speed until well blended. Add eggs and vanilla and beat to combine.
2. In a small bowl, whisk together flour, baking powder, and salt.
3. Add about a quarter of the dry mixture at a time to chocolate mixture, mixing on low after each addition. Cover bowl with plastic wrap and chill for 2 hours.
4. Preheat oven to 350°F. and line two baking sheets with parchment paper.
5. Shape dough into 1-inch balls and roll in confectioners' sugar. Place 2 inches apart on prepared baking sheet and bake for 10 minutes, until firm around the edges. Let cool on the pan for 5 minutes, then transfer to a wire rack to cool completely.

Do-ahead: *Cookies can be made 1 days ahead. Store in an airtight container.*

Do-ahead: *Whoopie pies can be made 4 days ahead. Store in an airtight container in the refrigerator.*

Whoopie Pies

Makes 22

It's called a pie but it's shaped like cookie, with the fluff of a cake. Its origins are murky—New England and Pennsylvania both claim to be its birthplace and it's the official state treat of Maine, which also hosts the Whoopie Pie Festival. But no matter what it is (cake, pie, cookie) or where it comes from, what I do know is that our customers can't get enough. For people who already love the cakiness of our black-and-whites, a whoopie pie—two mini chocolate cakes sandwiched with tangy cream cheese frosting—takes it to the next level.

Cakes:

1 cup all-purpose flour
1¼ cups cake flour
¼ cup cocoa powder
1¼ teaspoons baking soda
1 teaspoon espresso powder
1 teaspoon kosher salt
1½ sticks butter, softened
1¼ cups sugar
2 eggs
½ teaspoon vanilla extract
1 cup buttermilk

Filling:

1 pound cream cheese, softened
4 sticks butter, softened
2 cups confectioners' sugar
1 teaspoon vanilla extract
½ teaspoon salt

1. **Make the cakes:** Preheat oven to 350°F and line two baking sheets with parchment paper. In a medium bowl, whisk together the flours, cocoa powder, baking soda, espresso powder, and salt. In the bowl of a stand mixer or working with electric beaters in a large bowl, cream together the butter and sugar on medium-high speed until light and fluffy, 4 to 5 minutes, scraping down the bowl occasionally. Beat in the eggs and vanilla until well combined. Reduce speed to low and add dry ingredients in thirds, alternating with buttermilk in two additions, until you have a smooth batter.
2. Using a 1-ounce (2 tablespoon) ice cream scoop or a tablespoon, drop 2-tablespoon mounds of batter onto the baking sheet, placing 3 inches apart.
3. Bake 10 to 12 minutes, until they spring back to the touch. Let cool on pan 5 minutes, then use a spatula to transfer the cookies to rack to cool completely.
4. **Make the filling:** In the bowl of a stand mixer or working with electric beaters in a large bowl, cream all the ingredients together on medium-high speed until smooth and fluffy, 4 to 5 minutes.
5. **Assemble the pies:** Spread or pipe filling on flat side of one cake and sandwich with another.

Sliceable and Shareable:

Brownies and Bars, Tarts and Pies

Cocoa Brownies

Makes one 8-inch pan

This is an old reliable in our bakery case, a real standard that's packed for picnics, shipped off in care packages, and devoured right on the spot. We use cocoa powder to deliver the deepest chocolate flavor and densest, fudgiest texture. They're easiest to cut when cool, but hard to resist when still warm and, as my daughter Alison prefers, with a big scoop of ice cream.

1 stick unsalted butter, plus more for the pan
1 cup sugar
1½ teaspoons pure vanilla extract
2 large eggs, room temperature
½ cup flour
½ cup unsweetened cocoa powder
¼ teaspoon baking powder
¼ teaspoon kosher salt
½ cup chopped walnuts or pecans, optional

1. Preheat the oven to 350°F. Butter an 8-inch square cake pan and line it with parchment paper, leaving overhang on two opposite sides. In a large saucepan, melt the butter over low heat. Remove from the heat and allow to cool slightly. Stir in the sugar and vanilla until blended, then stir in the eggs until incorporated. Add the flour, cocoa, baking powder, and salt and mix until combined. Fold in the walnuts if using. Spread the batter evenly in the prepared pan.
2. Bake until set, 20 to 25 minutes. Cool on a wire rack, then remove from pan and cut into 2- to 3-inch squares.

Do-ahead: *The brownies can be kept in an airtight container at room temperature for up to 1 week, in the refrigerator for up to 1 month, or in the freezer for up to 3 months.*

Do-ahead: *Bars can be made 5 days ahead. Store in an airtight container in the refrigerator.*

Cheesecake Brownies

Makes one 8-inch pan

I'm not a chocoholic, but there's something about the addition of tangy cream cheese that cuts through its richness and makes it irresistible, even to me. I channeled the classic black-bottom cupcakes—chocolate cake with pockets of cream cheese studded with chocolate chips—and added this brownie to our menu to complete our brownie bunch (which also includes Caramel Swirl, page 39, and Rocky Road, page 43, as well as M&M—no recipe necessary, you can imagine how we make these!). These brownies, with their marbled tops, are as beautiful as they are delicious—they're sure to receive high praise at any bake sale.

Brownie batter:

1½ sticks butter, cut into pieces
5 ounces semisweet chocolate, roughly chopped
3 eggs
1 cups granulated sugar
½ cup dark brown sugar
1 teaspoons vanilla extract
¼ teaspoon kosher salt
1 cup cake flour

Cheesecake swirl:

8 ounces cream cheese, softened
½ cup granulated sugar
1 egg
½ teaspoon vanilla extract

1. **Make the brownie batter:** Preheat oven to 375°F. Butter an 8-inch square baking pan and line it with parchment paper, leaving overhang on two opposite sides.
2. Melt butter and chocolate in a double boiler or in a heatproof bowl in the microwave in 20-second increments. Set aside to cool slightly.
3. Working with a stand mixer fitted with the whisk attachment or using electric beaters and a large bowl, beat the eggs with sugars, vanilla, and salt and mix on medium-high speed until pale in color and slightly more voluminous, 4 to 5 minutes. Stir in melted chocolate mixture to combine.
4. Sift in the flour over the bowl and fold to gently incorporate, stopping as soon as no dry streaks remain.
5. **Make the cheesecake swirl:** In the bowl of a stand mixer fitted with a paddle attachment or working with electric beaters and a medium bowl, beat the cream cheese on medium speed until light and fluffy.
6. Add the sugar and beat until the sugar is dissolved, 2 to 3 minutes. Beat in the egg and vanilla until combined.
7. Spread the brownie batter into the prepared pan, then dollop the cheesecake batter over top. Use a knife to gently swirl the two together.
8. Bake for 45 to 50 minutes, until a toothpick comes out clean.
9. Cool completely in pan on a rack, then use parchment handles to transfer to a cutting board and slice into 16 squares.

Caramel Swirl Brownies

Makes one 8-inch pan

These days, there's a food holiday (or ten) for every day of the year. Some are silly—national mince meat pie day? national bologna day?—but others are fun excuses to try something new at the bakery. One year, to "celebrate" National Brownie Day (a.k.a. December 8), we sold brownies with sweet caramel sauce twisted into the batter. They caught on—now we have to sell them all the time, holiday or not.

Caramel:

½ cup sugar
3 tablespoons water
⅓ cup heavy cream, room temperature
2 tablespoons butter, softened
1 teaspoon vanilla extract
¼ teaspoon kosher salt
¼ cup flour

Brownies:

6 ounces semisweet chocolate, chopped
6 tablespoons butter
1½ tablespoons unsweetened cocoa powder
2 eggs
1 cup sugar
1 teaspoon vanilla extract
¾ cup plus 2 tablespoons flour
¼ teaspoon baking powder
½ teaspoon kosher salt

1. **Make the caramel:** In a medium saucepan over medium heat, cook the sugar and water, stirring constantly, until the sugar is dissolved.
2. Increase the heat to medium-high and bring to a boil. Cook undisturbed until it turns an amber color, about 5 to 6 minutes.
3. Remove from heat and whisk in the cream (mixture will bubble dramatically). Add the butter, vanilla, and salt and stir until smooth.
4. Transfer to a bowl and chill the caramel for 2 hours, stirring occasionally, until caramel is thick and cool. Stir in the flour.
5. **Make the brownies:** Preheat oven to 350°F. Butter an 8-inch square cake pan and line it with parchment paper, leaving overhang on two opposite sides.
6. In a double boiler or in a medium bowl in the microwave working in 20-second increments, melt the chocolate and butter together and stir until smooth. Whisk in the cocoa and let cool.
7. In a large bowl, whisk together the eggs, sugar, and vanilla until just combined.
8. In a medium bowl, whisk together the flour, baking powder, and salt.

(Continued on next page)

9. Add the chocolate mixture to the egg mixture and whisk to combine. Fold in the flour mixture until no dry streaks remain. Pour into prepared pan.
10. Pipe the caramel over the brownie batter. Optionally use a butter knife or offset spatula to swirl some into the batter.
11. Bake 30 to 40 minutes, until set in the center.
12. Cool on a wire rack for an hour, then remove from pan and let cool completely on a wire rack before cutting into squares.

Do-ahead: *Caramel without flour can be covered and refrigerated for two weeks. Warm slightly over low heat or heat in 20-second increments in the microwave before using. Brownies can be made 3 to 4 days ahead. Store in an airtight container.*

Passover Walnut Brownies

Makes one 8-inch pan

People who observe Passover are always looking for something tasty to eat for dessert. These go above and beyond in deliciousness. They're really dense and fudgy with a deep chocolate flavor enhanced by a shot of coffee. Be sure to buy matzoh cake meal, not just matzoh meal, for the fudgiest brownies.

1 cup butter or Kosher-for-Passover margarine, plus more for the pan
1½ cups granulated sugar
½ cup packed light brown sugar
¾ cup unsweetened cocoa powder
3 large eggs, room temperature
1 tablespoon brewed coffee
1 cup matzoh cake meal
½ teaspoon salt
½ cup finely chopped toasted walnuts, optional

1. Preheat the oven to 350°F. Grease an 8-inch square cake pan with butter or margarine and line it with parchment paper, leaving overhang on two opposite sides.
2. Melt the butter in a large saucepan over medium heat, stirring to evenly melt. Remove from the heat and add both sugars. Stir until well combined. Sift the cocoa into the saucepan and stir until incorporated. While stirring, add the eggs and then the coffee. When the mixture is smooth, add the matzoh cake meal and salt, stirring just until no traces of meal remain. Fold in the walnuts if using. Scrape the batter into the prepared pan, smoothing the top.
3. Bake until the top is set and a toothpick inserted in the center comes out almost clean, 25 to 30 minutes.
4. Cool in the pan on a wire rack. Remove from pan, cut into squares, and serve.

Do-ahead: *The brownies can be kept in an airtight container for up to 1 week, in the refrigerator for up to 1 month, or in the freezer for up to 3 months.*

Rocky Road Brownies

Makes one 8-inch pan

Inspired by the classic ice cream flavor, these brownies are studded with walnuts and topped with a cobbled layer of semi-melted marshmallows and chocolate chips. They're more cakey than our other brownies—a lighter, fluffier brownie for those times when you're ready for a change from the ultra-rich and fudgy.

½ cup flour
¼ teaspoon baking powder
¼ teaspoon kosher salt
¼ cup butter
2 ounces semisweet chocolate
2 eggs
½ cup sugar
¾ teaspoon vanilla extract
¼ cup walnuts, chopped
1 cup miniature marshmallows
½ cup semisweet chocolate chips

1. Preheat oven to 350°F.
2. Butter an 8-inch baking pan and line with parchment paper, leaving overhang on opposite sides.
3. In a medium bowl, whisk together the flour, baking powder, and salt.
4. In a double boiler or in a heatproof bowl in the microwave in 20-second increments, melt the butter and chocolate together and stir until smooth. Remove from heat and cool slightly, about 5 minutes. Whisk in the eggs, sugar, and vanilla. Add the flour mixture and whisk until no streaks remain. Stir in the walnuts and transfer to prepared baking sheet.
5. Bake 25 to 30 minutes, until a toothpick comes out with moist crumbs attached.
6. Remove from the oven and sprinkle with marshmallows and chocolate chips.
7. Return to the oven for 4 to 5 minutes, until the chips and marshmallows melt over the brownies.
8. Cool completely in pan on a rack, then use parchment handles to transfer to a cutting board and slice into 16 squares.

Do-ahead: *Brownies can be made 4 days ahead. Store in an airtight container at room temperature.*

Lemon Bars

Makes 12 bars

Perfect for summer (or for the middle of winter when you're dreaming of summer), these puckery bars taste like edible lemonade. When I was developing the recipe for the menu, I was aiming for a lemon bar that was super tart, with a soft, tender base that would meld with the smooth and luscious lemon custard topping. The end result? My favorite lemon bar to date.

Crust:

2 sticks unsalted butter, cold, cut into small pieces
2 cups flour
½ cup light brown sugar
½ teaspoon kosher salt

Filling:

4 eggs
1½ cups granulated sugar
¾ cup lemon juice
⅓ cup flour
3 tablespoons confectioners' sugar

1. Preheat oven to 350°F. Line a 13 x 9 x 2-inch baking pan with parchment paper, leaving overhang on the long sides to make it easier to remove the bars later on.
2. **Make the crust:** Add butter, flour, brown sugar, and salt to the bowl of a food processor.
3. Pulse until mixture begins to form small lumps, about 1 minute.
4. Sprinkle dough into prepared pan and use the pads of your fingers to press evenly into the bottom. Poke the dough all over with the tines of a fork, then bake until golden, about 20 minutes. Reduce oven to 300°F.
5. When the crust is almost finished baking, **make the filling:** Whisk together eggs and granulated sugar in a medium bowl until well combined. Add the lemon juice and flour and whisk until smooth. Pour mixture over the hot crust, then bake until set, about 30 minutes.
6. Let cool completely in the pan, then use parchment handles to remove, using an offset spatula or butter knife to detach any sticky bits. Sift confectioners' sugar over top and slice into 12 bars.

Do-ahead: *Bars can be made 3 to 4 days ahead. Store in an airtight container in the refrigerator.*

Rainbow Cookies

Makes 24 cookies

Don't be fooled by the name—rainbow "cookies" are really small stacks of spongy and light almond-flavored cake with layers of jam and a coat of chocolate. Making three cakes in different shades is less of a production than you'd think, since each one is made from the same batter, then divided up and colored. Use whatever flavor of jam you'd like (as long as it's smooth) and try not to be discouraged if your stack of cakes looks messy at first—once you weigh it down (and give it some time in the refrigerator), you'll be able to slice it into neat pieces. Just make sure you've cleared enough space in the fridge before you get started!

2 cups flour
½ teaspoon salt
3 sticks butter, softened
8 ounces almond paste (not marzipan)
1 cup sugar
4 eggs
¼ teaspoon almond extract
Red and green food coloring
Smooth apricot jam, warmed slightly to a runny consistency
5 ounces bittersweet chocolate

1. Preheat oven to 350°F. and line three 13 x 9-inch baking pans with parchment paper, leaving overhang on the long sides. (If you don't have three pans, you can bake the cakes in batches, leaving the waiting batter at room temperature.)
2. In a small bowl, whisk together the flour and salt.
3. In the bowl of stand mixer fitted with a paddle attachment or working with electric beaters and a large bowl, cream together the butter, almond paste, and sugar on medium speed until light and fluffy, 4 to 5 minutes.
4. Add the eggs one at a time, scraping down the sides of the bowl between additions, and then the almond extract.
5. Reduce speed to low and add the flour mixture and beat to combine. You'll have a dough that resembles a thick cake batter.
6. Remove two-thirds of the dough. Spread one third into one of the prepared pans and transfer the other third to a small bowl. Add red food coloring to the portion in the mixer and beat to combine, adding more color until you've reached the desired hue. Transfer to the second prepared pan and spread evenly. Wipe out the mixer, add the remaining third batter, and color with green food coloring. Transfer to the last prepared pan.

(Continued on next page)

7. Bake 12 to 15 minutes, or until a toothpick comes out clean. Place the pans on a rack to cool for a few minutes and then remove the cakes from the pans. Transfer to wire racks to cool completely.
8. Once cakes are cool, line a rimmed sheet pan with foil. Place red layer on the foil and use a pastry brush to spread a very thin layer of warm apricot jam on top. Place uncolored layer on top of that, spread with jam, and top with final green layer.
9. Cover the cake with foil and top with a sheet pan. Place heavy cans on top of the sheet pan—this will compress the cake. Refrigerate for at least 6 hours.
10. Melt the chocolate in a double boiler or in 20-second increments in the microwave. Spread the chocolate over the cake and along the sides and let set, about 30 minutes.
11. Cut the cake into 24 pieces (6 x 4), dipping the knife in hot water between slices.

Do-ahead: *Cake can be made 1 week ahead. Store in an airtight container in the fridge.*

Somewhere Over the Rainbow

I've been drawn to rainbow cookies—which are sometimes called rainbow bars, rainbow cake, flag cookies, Napoleon cookies, seven-layer cookies, or tri-color cookies—ever since I was a little girl. And I'll clear up any confusion in regards to cookie versus bar versus cake—despite the moniker, a rainbow cookie is really a slice of a three-layer sponge cake.

There is something so eye-catching about their color-blocked appearance: three fat stripes of red, yellow, and green, delineated with thin smears of raspberry jam. A familiar staple at synagogue functions, event dessert stations, and in the display case of every bakery in New York City we frequented, I always knew a rainbow cookie would be tasty. Even if the cake were dry or crumbly, the jam, almond paste, and chocolate coating would redeem it.

Even though I've known rainbow cookies to be a fixture of Jewish-American baking, it turns out they are just as iconic—if not more so—in the city's Italian-American sweet shops. Rainbow cookies don't seem to have a direct Italian counterpart, causing historians to surmise that immigrants created the treat, perhaps to pay homage to the Italian flag (hence, "flag cookies") or to recreate a homeland dessert with the ingredients they had access to in America. The confections peaked in popularity in the late nineteenth and early twentieth centuries and, to this date, are still popular on Long Island, where Mr. Greenberg grew up and, likely, where he had his first taste.

There's clearly a synergy between Jewish and Italian baking. We've both got biscotti (mandelbread!), butter cookies in all shapes and sizes, and the always irresistible rainbow cookies, just to name a few examples. It just goes to show that good taste, and lots of sugar, transcends cultures.

We sell the rainbow cookies all year round, and have added a white chocolate covered version that is sinful, especially for our customers looking to scratch a nostalgic itch, but they're in highest demand during the winter holidays when they make for a beloved gift or an impressive contribution to the dessert exchange.

Three Berry Tart

Makes one 9-inch tart

We make a lot of different fruit tarts at the bakery, but there's something special about the three berry tart that makes it the most popular. Perhaps it's because it's the most photogenic, with those bright berries like sparkling jewels covering the smooth pastry cream. It's best during the summer, when berries are ripe and sweet, but it makes for an elegant dinner party dessert year-round. And while the berries are particularly beautiful, feel free to swap in whatever fruit you prefer: thinly sliced mango or kiwi, halved sugar plums or grapes, peach or apricot wedges, or even grapefruit segments.

Dough:

3 tablespoons slivered blanched almonds
6 tablespoons sugar
1¼ cups flour
¼ teaspoon salt
6 tablespoons unsalted butter, cold and cut into 6 pieces

Pastry cream:

1 cup milk
½ cup heavy cream
⅔ cup sugar, divided
¼ teaspoon vanilla extract
¼ teaspoon kosher salt
3 tablespoons cornstarch
2 egg yolks
2 eggs
4 tablespoons butter, room temperature, cut into pieces

Assembly:

1 cup raspberries
⅓ cup blueberries
¾ cup whole strawberries, hulled, or blackberries

1. Preheat the oven to 350°F.
2. **Make the dough:** Pulse the almonds in a food processor until finely ground. Add sugar, flour, and salt, and pulse until combined. Add butter and pulse until coarse crumbs form without large butter clumps.
3. Transfer dough into a 9-inch tart pan with removable bottom, then use the back of a measuring cup to press it evenly and firmly across the bottom and up the sides. Poke all over with the tines of a fork. Butter a piece of parchment paper and place buttered side down in the tart shell. Fill

(Continued on next page)

with pie weights, dried beans, or rice, making sure the weights are pushed all the way to the edges and at least part-way up the sides. Bake until golden and firm to touch, about 30 minutes. Carefully remove parchment and pie weights. Bake for an additional 10 to 15 minutes, until golden. Transfer pan to a wire rack and let cool completely.

4. **Make the pastry cream:** In a medium saucepan, whisk together milk, heavy cream, half the sugar, vanilla, and salt. Bring to a boil over low heat.
5. In a small bowl, combine the remaining sugar, cornstarch, egg yolks, and eggs.
6. While constantly whisking, use a ladle to slowly stream in about ¼ cup of the hot milk mixture into your egg mixture. Add more hot milk from the pot, continuing to whisk constantly, until the egg mixture is warm to touch. Now slowly return the milk egg mixture to the pot, whisking constantly. Return the mixture to a boil, then whisk vigorously over low heat for 2 full minutes; the pastry cream should be thick and smooth. Pour through a fine-mesh sieve into a heatproof bowl.
7. Add the butter and whisk until thoroughly blended. Press a piece of plastic wrap directly on the surface and refrigerate until ready to use.
8. **Assemble the tart:** Whisk the pastry cream to loosen it up, then transfer to the tart shell, being sure to cover the whole bottom and get at least halfway up the sides. (You can add more or less pastry cream according to your taste). Place raspberries around the outside perimeter, followed by a circle of blueberries and a second circle of raspberries. Fill in the center with strawberries or blackberries.
9. Refrigerate until ready to serve.

Do-ahead: *Pastry cream can be made up to 2 days ahead. Transfer to an airtight container, press a piece of plastic wrap to the surface, and store in the refrigerator.*

Do-ahead: *Tart, without whipped topping, can be made 1 day ahead. Store covered in the refrigerator.*

Chocolate Ganache Tart

Makes one 9-inch tart

Our customers must not know how simple it is to make this elegant tart—otherwise, they'd all be baking it at home instead of stopping at William Greenberg to pick one up on the way to their dinner parties! Lucky for us, the secret's not out (yet). The crust—particularly tender thanks to the addition of ground almonds—is filled with a smooth, creamy ganache that tastes like a better version of your favorite chocolate bar. Be sure to splurge for high-quality chocolate for this recipe; with so few other ingredients, it really makes a difference. If you want to dress up the tart, top it with fresh berries.

Tart shell:

3 tablespoons slivered blanched almonds
6 tablespoons sugar
1¼ cups flour
¼ teaspoon kosher salt
6 tablespoons unsalted butter, cold and cut into 6 pieces

Ganache filling:

12 ounces bittersweet chocolate, chopped
1¼ cups heavy cream
¼ teaspoon kosher salt
1 teaspoon vanilla extract

Whipped cream topping:

1 cup heavy cream, cold
2 tablespoons sugar
¼ teaspoon vanilla extract

1. Preheat oven to 350°F. Place a large bowl or the bowl of a stand mixer in the refrigerator to chill.
2. To make the dough, pulse the almonds in a food processor until finely ground. Add sugar, flour, and salt and pulse until combined. Add butter and pulse until coarse crumbs form without large butter clumps.
3. Transfer dough into a 9-inch tart pan with removable bottom, then use the back of a measuring cup to press it evenly and firmly across the bottom and up the sides. Poke all over with the tines of a fork. Butter a piece of parchment paper and place buttered side down in the tart shell. Fill with pie weights, dried beans, or rice, making sure the weights are pushed all the way to the edges and at least part-way up the sides. Bake until golden and firm to touch, about 30 minutes. Carefully remove parchment and pie weights. Bake for an additional 10 to 15 minutes, until golden. Transfer pan to a wire rack and let cool completely.
4. To make the ganache, place chocolate in large mixing bowl. In a saucepan, bring cream and salt to a boil. Pour hot cream over chocolate. Stir until smooth, then add vanilla.
5. Pour chocolate mixture into cooled tart shell. Let stand about 2 hours, or chill 1 hour, until set.
6. When ready to serve, beat cream, sugar, and vanilla in the chilled bowl until stiff peaks form. Pipe or dollop around the tart's inside edge.

Do-ahead: *Pie can be made 1 day ahead. Cover with foil and store at room temperature until ready to serve. Dough can be refrigerated for 2 days or frozen for 2 months. If frozen, defrost overnight in the refrigerator before rolling.*

Chocolate Pecan Pie

Makes one 9-inch pie

We only sell this pie at Thanksgiving time, but that's the beauty of a cookbook. You can make it for yourself anytime you want! The chocolate chips, which are simply mixed into our pecan pie filling, melt in the heat of the oven, creating a gooey, chocolate center that is a delicious alternative to our traditional version.

Dough:

1¼ cups flour
¼ cup sugar
½ teaspoon kosher salt
1 stick butter, cold, cut into pieces
¼ cup ice water

Filling:

¾ cup light brown sugar
¾ cup corn syrup
2 tablespoons bourbon
2 tablespoons flour
1 teaspoon vanilla extract
½ teaspoon kosher salt
3 tablespoons butter, melted
3 eggs, beaten
1½ cups pecan halves
½ cup mini semi-sweet chocolate chips

1. **Make the dough:** In a food processor, combine flour, sugar, and salt and pulse to combine.
2. Add the butter and pulse to break up into walnut-sized pieces. Gradually add the ice water and pulse until pea-sized clumps form.
3. Turn the dough out onto a floured surface and knead until a smooth, soft dough forms. If dough is dry, sprinkle over more ice water by the teaspoon until dry bits adhere.
4. Flatten dough into a disc, wrap in plastic, and refrigerate for at least two hours.
5. Preheat oven to 425°F. On a lightly floured surface roll dough into a 11-inch circle about ⅛-inch thick. Use your rolling pin to transfer the dough to a 9-inch pie plate. Poke all over with the tines of a fork and refrigerate for at least 30 minutes. Butter a piece of parchment paper and place buttered side down in the tart shell. Fill with pie weights, dried beans, or rice, making sure the weights are pushed all the way to the edges and at least part-way up the sides. Bake until golden and firm to touch, about 20 minutes. Carefully remove parchment and pie weights. Cool completely on wire rack.
6. **Make the pie:** Lower the oven temperature to 350°F.
7. In a large bowl, stir together brown sugar, corn syrup, bourbon, flour, vanilla, and salt until well combined. Add melted butter and eggs and stir to combine. Mix in pecans and chocolate chips.
8. Pour into cooled pie shell. Bake for about 45 to 60 minutes, until firm with just a slight jiggle in the center. Let cool completely before slicing.

On the Rise:
Quick and Yeast Breads

Sour Cream Blueberry Muffins

Makes 1 dozen

Our bakery's breakfast bestseller is also my daughter Emily's favorite morning treat. They make you feel like you're having dessert with your coffee. These muffins bake up big and very fluffy. Their nice melt-in-your-mouth texture is as soft as cake but bursting with fresh blueberries.

2 cups flour
1 tablespoon baking powder
¼ teaspoon salt
1 cup sugar
2 tablespoons butter, melted and cooled
1 egg
1½ cups sour cream
2 cups blueberries

1. Preheat the oven to 350°F. Line a standard muffin tin with paper liners. In a large bowl, whisk together the flour, baking powder, and salt. In a medium bowl, whisk the sugar, butter, egg, and sour cream until smooth. Pour over the flour and fold just until all traces of flour disappear. Fold in the blueberries until evenly distributed. Divide the batter among the muffin cups.
2. Bake until golden and a toothpick inserted in the center of one comes out clean, 20 to 25 minutes. Serve warm or cool to room temperature.

Do-ahead: *The muffins are best eaten the day they're made, but they can be frozen in an airtight container for up to 2 months and reheated in an oven or toaster oven.*

Corn Muffins

Makes 2 dozen

Mr. Greenberg was a muffin fiend—he added a whole array of muffins to the menu and we've kept them around for the loyal customers who are clued in to just how delicious they are. The corn muffins, perfectly sweet (but not overly so), are best enjoyed warm with butter and honey or jam. They're humble in appearance, which I consider an added bonus. Your friends and family won't know how tasty they are—and that means more for you.

1½ cups cornmeal
1½ cups flour
1½ tablespoons baking powder
½ teaspoon kosher salt
3 cups milk
4 eggs
2 sticks butter, softened
1 cup sugar

1. Preheat oven to 350°F. and line a standard muffin tin with paper liners.
2. In a small bowl, whisk together the cornmeal, flour, baking powder, and salt. In a liquid measuring cup, beat milk and eggs until well combined.
3. In a stand mixer fitted with the paddle attachment or working with electric beaters and a large bowl, cream together butter and sugar on medium speed until light and fluffy, 4 to 5 minutes. Reduce speed to low and add the flour mixture in thirds, alternating with the milk mixture in two additions, until you have a smooth batter.
4. Divide the batter among the muffin liners, filling each just over three-quarters of the way. Bake for 25 to 30 minutes, or until a toothpick comes out clean. Let cool completely in the pan.

Do-ahead: *Muffins can be made 3 days ahead. Store in an airtight container at room temperature.*

Cranberry Muffins

Makes 28 standard muffins

Cranberries are tart, tangy, and good for so much more than Thanksgiving sauce. These airy muffins are polka-dotted with their red bursts, adding a beautiful color and a sour-sweet flavor that blueberries don't deliver. While these muffins stay good for three days, they're really at their peak the day they're made. Since it can be hard to finish a whole batch in twenty-four hours (though not as hard as you'd imagine . . .), I recommend freezing the leftovers (or making a batch for the sole purpose of stocking the freezer). Let them thaw in the fridge overnight, then reheat them in a 300°F. oven or in the microwave until they're warm enough to make a pat of butter melt.

3½ cups flour
1½ cups sugar
5 teaspoons baking powder
½ teaspoon kosher salt
1½ cups milk
¼ cup sour cream
4 eggs
1 stick butter, melted
2 cups cranberries, fresh or frozen

1. Preheat oven to 375°F. and line two standard muffin tins with liners.
2. In a large bowl, whisk together the flour, sugar, baking powder, and salt.
3. In a separate large bowl, whisk together the milk, sour cream, eggs, and butter.
4. Add the dry ingredients to the wet ingredients and use a rubber spatula to stir until you have a smooth batter.
5. Fold in the cranberries.
6. Divide the batter into liners until three-quarters full.
7. Bake 20 to 25 minutes, or until muffins are golden brown and a toothpick comes out clean.
8. Cool in the tins 10 minutes and transfer to a rack to cool completely.

Do-ahead: *Muffins can be made 3 days ahead. Store in an airtight container.*

Double Chocolate Muffins

Makes 2 dozen

This is as close to a brownie as a muffin can get. And the best part? You can get away with eating it for breakfast. Even though they're packed with cocoa powder and chocolate chips, the texture is light and airy, placing them squarely in camp muffin (rather than camp cupcake). I recommend making these on the weekend so that you can grab one as you run out the door on a harried Tuesday morning. It'll be a very good reason to drag yourself out of bed.

2 cups flour
½ cup cocoa powder
2 teaspoons baking soda
¼ teaspoon kosher salt
¾ cup sugar
⅔ cup vegetable oil
⅔ cup milk
2 eggs
2 teaspoons vanilla extract
½ cup sour cream
1 cup chocolate chips

1. Preheat oven to 350°F. and line two standard muffin tins with liners.
2. In a small bowl, whisk together flour, cocoa powder, baking soda, and salt.
3. In a large bowl, whisk together sugar, oil, and milk until fully combined. Whisk in the eggs and vanilla until smooth. Whisk in sour cream until just combined.
4. Fold in the flour mixture until no dry spots remain, being careful not to overmix.
5. Add the chocolate chips and mix to combine.
6. Use a large spoon or ice cream scoop to fill the liners halfway.
7. Bake for 15 to 18 minutes, or until a toothpick comes out clean.
8. Cool in tin for about 5 minutes, then transfer to wire racks to cool completely.

Do-ahead: *Muffins can be made 3 to 4 days ahead. Store in an airtight container at room temperature.*

Raisin Scones

Makes 12

My ideal scone is very light and biscuit-like. It should melt on your tongue with little chewing involved and be just a touch sweet. It should taste great with jam or salted butter but not require it. The key to making great scones is to keep the dairy cold—cold butter and milk will make the dough easier to work with, which means you won't need to handle it as much. And the less you handle it, the more tender the scones will be. If you don't have a round cookie cutter, shape the dough into a round and cut it into triangular wedges.

- 2½ cups flour
- ½ cup plus 1 tablespoon sugar
- 1 tablespoon baking powder
- ¼ teaspoon kosher salt
- 1 stick butter, chilled and cut into pieces
- 1 egg, beaten, plus 1 egg, beaten for egg wash
- ½ teaspoon vanilla extract
- ⅔ cup milk, chilled
- 1 cup golden raisins

1. Combine flour, ½ cup sugar, baking powder, and salt in a food processor and pulse to combine.
2. Pulse in the chilled butter until pea- and walnut-sized clumps form, about 10 short pulses. Add the beaten egg and vanilla and pulse 4 times to combine. Pour in the milk and pulse just until you have a sticky, loosely-held-together dough, 10 to 12 short pulses. Stir in the raisins with a spoon or spatula, then transfer to a lightly floured work surface. Lightly flour the dough and knead a few times, adding more flour if it's too sticky. Pat into a thick disc, wrap with plastic wrap, and chill for at least 30 minutes.
3. Preheat oven to 375°F and line two baking sheets with parchment paper.
4. On a floured surface, roll out the dough to ½ inch thick.
5. Punch out scones using a 3-inch round cookie cutter. Place scones 2 inches apart on prepared baking sheets. Reroll any scraps and punch out remaining scones.
6. Brush scones with egg wash and sprinkle with remaining 1 tablespoon sugar.
7. Bake for 15 to 20 minutes, or until golden. Cool scones slightly on the baking sheets, then transfer to racks to cool completely or eat warm with butter and honey.

Do-ahead: *Dough can be made 1 day in advance. Keep chilled in the refrigerator. Scones can be made 2 to 3 days ahead. Store in an airtight container at room temperature.*

Honey Loaf

Makes 2 loaves

I only use the word "moist" to describe cake when I really mean it. This is one such case. Heady with warm fall spices and sweetened with honey, this cake is dense and delectable. It's especially popular around Rosh Hashanah when we eat apples and honey to symbolize the sweetness of the new year. To make this dessert parve, simply swap in 4 additional tablespoons of vegetable oil to replace the butter.

3 cups flour
1 tablespoon baking powder
1 teaspoon baking soda
2 teaspoon cinnamon
½ teaspoon allspice
¼ teaspoon ground ginger
¼ teaspoon kosher salt
4 eggs, beaten
1¾ cups honey
1 cup black coffee, cooled
¾ cup dark brown sugar
1 stick butter, melted and slightly cooled
¼ cup vegetable oil
1 cup chopped nuts-walnuts or pecans

1. Preheat oven to 350°F. Grease two 9x5-inch loaf pans with butter or nonstick cooking spray, then line with parchment paper, leaving overhang on the long sides.
2. In a large bowl, whisk together flour, baking powder, baking soda, cinnamon, allspice, ginger, and salt.
3. Add eggs, honey, coffee, sugar, butter, and oil. Using a wood spoon, stir until smooth but don't go wild: You want to incorporate the dry ingredients without overmixing. Stir in nuts.
4. Divide batter between the two prepared pans.
5. Bake for 45 to 50 minutes or until toothpick comes out clean.
6. Cool in pan on racks for 15 minutes.
7. Remove from pan using parchment overhang and continue to cool on rack.

Do-ahead: *These are even better the second day and can be stored wrapped in foil for 6 days.*

Do-ahead: *Cake can be made 5 days ahead. Cover with foil and store and room temperature.*

Lemon Pound Cake

Makes 2 loaves

We do sell this pound cake by the slice, but most people choose to buy it by the loaf. It's one of those anytime snacking cakes that's perfect for having around the kitchen—you'll have a sliver with your morning coffee, another with your afternoon tea, and a slice (or two) before calling it a day. Dress it up for company by serving it with soft whipped cream and fresh fruit. This recipe makes two loaves so that you can keep one for yourself and share the other with friends and loved ones. And if you prefer orange to lemon, simply swap out lemon juice for orange juice and lemon extract for pure orange extract. If you can't find lemon or orange extract, use 1 tablespoon of finely grated zest in its place. Don't have two 8x4 loaf pans? Use two 9x5 pans—just know that your cakes will be a little shorter.

2 cups flour
2 teaspoons baking powder
¼ teaspoon kosher salt
2 sticks butter, softened
1½ cups sugar
4 eggs
½ teaspoon lemon extract (or 1 tablespoon lemon zest)
¼ teaspoon vanilla extract
1 cup confectioners' sugar, sifted
2 teaspoons lemon zest
¼ cup lemon juice
Yellow food coloring, optional

1. Preheat oven to 325°F. Grease two 8x4-inch loaf pans with butter and line with parchment paper, leaving overhang on both of the long sides. Butter the parchment.
2. In a small bowl, whisk together the flour, baking powder, and salt.
3. In the bowl of a stand mixer fitted with a paddle attachment or working with electric beaters and a large bowl, cream together the butter and sugar on medium speed until light and fluffy, 4 to 5 minutes, scraping down the sides of the bowl occasionally. Add the eggs, one by one, beating to incorporate after each addition and scraping down the sides of the bowl. Add the lemon extract (or zest) and vanilla and beat to combine.
4. Reduce the speed to low and gradually add the flour mixture, beating just until incorporated.
5. Divide batter between prepared pans and bake 45-50 minutes or until a toothpick comes out clean.
6. Cool on a rack for 15 minutes, then use parchment handles to remove loaves to wire racks to cool completely.
7. When cake is cool, mix together the confectioners' sugar, lemon zest, and lemon juice, starting with 3 tablespoons and adding more as needed until you have a thick but pourable consistency. Optionally add a few drops of yellow food coloring for a more intense color or leave as is—it tastes delicious either way. Pour over the cakes and let set, about 30 minutes.

Chocolate Chip Pound Cake

Makes 1 Bundt

We're all about the classics at William Greenberg—not every dessert has to be a newfangled showstopper. This pound cake—dense, buttery, and punctuated with chocolate chips—is old-fashioned in the best way possible and a thick wedge makes for the ultimate afternoon treat.

2 cups flour
2 teaspoons baking powder
½ teaspoon kosher salt
2 sticks butter, room temperature
1½ cups sugar
4 eggs
½ teaspoon vanilla extract
1 cup chocolate chips

1. Preheat oven to 325°F. Grease a 9-cup Bundt pan with nonstick cooking spray and coat with flour, tapping to remove excess.
2. In a small bowl, whisk together the flour, baking powder, and salt.
3. In the bowl of a stand mixer fitted with a paddle attachment or working with electric beaters and a large bowl, cream together the butter and sugar on medium speed until light and fluffy, 4 to 5 minutes, scraping down the sides of the bowl occasionally.
4. Add the eggs one at a time, beating to incorporate after each addition and scraping down the sides of the mixer, until you have a smooth mixture. Add the vanilla and beat to combine.
5. Reduce the speed to low and gradually add the flour mixture, beating just until no dry spots remain. Stir in the chocolate chips.
6. Scrape the batter into the prepared pan.
7. Bake 55 to 60 minutes, or until a toothpick comes out clean.
8. Cool Bundt in pan for 15 minutes, then invert onto a wire rack to cool completely.

Do-ahead: *Wrapped in foil, the cake will keep at room temperature for 3 days.*

Challah

Makes 1 loaf

Even though I rely on my stand mixer to knead the dough these days, I used to knead the dough by hand for the zen-like experience. If you are willing to put in a bit of elbow grease, you can, too. You can also fill the dough with whatever you like—raisins, chocolate chips, nuts, dried cranberries, apples and cinnamon—or leave it plain, as I often do. For the high holidays, our traditional braided loaves are replaced with ones rolled into a round. The recipe below makes one loaf, but you can double, triple, or even quadruple it to make more.

½ cup plus 1 tablespoon warm water (105 to 115°F), divided
1½ teaspoons sugar, divided
1 envelope active dry yeast (2¼ teaspoons/7 grams)
3 cups flour, divided, plus more as needed
⅓ cup vegetable oil, plus more as needed
2 tablespoons honey
1½ teaspoons kosher salt
3 large eggs, divided
½ cup raisins, preferably a mixture of dark and golden, optional

1. Whisk ¼ cup of the warm water and 1 teaspoon of the sugar in a small bowl. Sprinkle the yeast over and let stand until the mixture is foamy, about 10 minutes. Meanwhile, sift 2¾ cups of the flour into the bowl of stand mixer fitted with the dough hook. Make a deep well in the center of the flour and pour in the oil, honey, salt, 2 of the eggs, the remaining ¼ cup plus 1 tablespoon water, the remaining ½ teaspoon sugar, and the yeast mixture. Mix on medium speed until a soft, sticky dough forms, about 4 minutes, scraping the bowl occasionally. Add the remaining ¼ cup flour and continue mixing until a soft, elastic dough ball forms and pulls away from the bottom of the bowl, about 4 more minutes. If the dough still feels sticky after the flour has been kneaded in, add a little more flour at a time until the dough is no longer sticky. Alternatively, sift the flour onto a large, clean work surface and make a deep well. Add the oil, honey, salt, two of the eggs, the remaining ¼ cup plus 1 tablespoon water, the remaining ½ teaspoon sugar, and the yeast mixture. Mix with your hands, gradually drawing the flour into the well. Once all the flour is incorporated, knead the dough, adding more flour as needed to form an elastic, soft dough ball.

(Continued on next page)

2. Oil a large bowl. Put the dough in the bowl and turn to coat with the oil. Cover the bowl loosely with plastic wrap and let rise in a warm spot until doubled in bulk, about 1 hour and 15 minutes. Uncover and punch down the dough. Cover and let rise again until doubled in bulk, about 1 hour longer. Rinse the raisins and pat dry. Oil a large baking sheet. Lightly flour a work surface. Punch down the dough and turn out onto the floured surface. Pat the dough into a 9 x 12-inch rectangle. Sprinkle the raisins over the dough. Roll up the rectangle as you would a jelly roll, then cut into three even pieces. Roll each piece into a rope about 18 inches long, then braid the ropes. Place on the prepared baking sheet. Cover with a slightly damp clean kitchen towel. Let rise until doubled, about 1 hour.
3. Position a rack in the center of the oven and preheat the oven to 375°F. Beat the remaining egg with a teaspoon of water. Brush the egg wash all over the risen loaf.
4. Bake for 15 minutes. Reduce the oven temperature to 350°F. and continue baking until the loaf sounds hollow when it's tapped on the bottom, about 25 minutes. Cool completely on a wire rack.

Do-ahead: *The challah is best the day it's made, but leftovers, wrapped in foil, are delicious as French toast or in bread pudding.*

It Started with Challah

Though I didn't know it at the time, my baking career started with challah. Every Friday, I'd make at least three batches of my signature loaf—which is sweeter than other versions and almost cake-like in its tenderness—to unwind at the end of a long week. There was something so peaceful and calming about kneading and shaping the dough and something so rewarding about sitting down to shabbat dinner and tearing off pieces of my own fluffy homemade bread.

I would give loaves to neighbors who caught whiffs of the intoxicating scent of fresh bread wafting out of my apartment as well as friends and family. A dear friend convinced me to launch a baking business and I opened Bread and Batter, which I operated in the hours when I wasn't busy with my day job in the wine and spirits industry. Soon word got out and not only was I supplying the neighbors in 12C but local restaurants and caterers as well, and Bread and Batter moved to the kitchen at the JCC. Before long, they asked for cheesecake, biscotti, and anything else I could whip up and I wasn't just in the challah business anymore.

But as much as I loved my small business, I yearned to grow and turn it into a brick-and-mortar retail shop. So when I was presented with the opportunity to purchase the bakery in 2008, I knew I couldn't pass it up.

I couldn't wait to be a part of the lives of so many customers—to serve them the desserts and baked goods that will remind them of happy memories and inspire the creation of new ones. And I have my challah to thank. When I watch customers line up around the block on Rosh Hashanah and other holidays to pick up their pre-ordered loaves from the truck we park outside the shop, I am thrilled to think that they are going to bring the challah into their homes and make it a part of their ritual. My challah will be a small part of their lives—perhaps they will associate its buttery, sweet softness with laughter around the dinner table or Sunday morning French toast—just as William Greenberg's desserts are wound into my own memories.

Schnecken

Makes 12 rolls

These yeasted sweet rolls—which are filled with cinnamon sugar and topped with a crunchy-sticky mix of maple syrup, chopped pecans, and raisins—are the German parent of the sticky bun, and they've been on the menu since day one. They're in highest demand on Thanksgiving and Christmas, when families like to start a big day of cooking with a sweet treat or unwrap presents as they unwind the swirl buns. Since the dough rises in the fridge overnight, all you have to do in the morning is shape and bake the buns. Your schnecken will be ready before the rest of the house stirs.

Dough:

3¼ cups flour
1 envelope active dry yeast (2¼ teaspoons/7 grams)
2 tablespoons granulated sugar
½ teaspoon kosher salt
½ cup milk
4 tablespoons butter
2 eggs
¼ cup sour cream

Topping:

1 stick butter, softened
¼ cup light brown sugar
2 tablespoons light corn syrup
¼ cup maple syrup
1¼ cup pecans, chopped
1 cup raisins

Filling:

½ cup light brown sugar
¼ cup granulated sugar
2 teaspoons cinnamon

1. **Make the dough:** In the bowl of a stand mixer fitted with a dough hook, combine the flour, yeast, granulated sugar, and salt.
2. In a small saucepan over low heat or in a small bowl in the microwave, warm the milk and butter until the butter has melted. In a small bowl, gently beat eggs. Gradually add the warm milk mixture, whisking constantly.
3. Add the butter mixture and sour cream to the mixer and knead for about 5 minutes on medium speed until the dough is pulling cleanly away from the bottom of the bowl. Use your hands to shape the dough into a ball, then place in a greased bowl, cover with plastic wrap, and refrigerate overnight or at least 8 hours.
4. **Make the topping:** In the bowl of a stand mixer fitted with a paddle attachment or working with electric beaters and a large bowl, beat the butter on medium speed until light and creamy and then add the light brown sugar and beat until combined, 1 to 2 minutes. Beat in the corn syrup and maple syrup followed by the pecans and raisins.
5. **Make the filling:** In a small bowl, mix together the light brown sugar granulated sugar, and cinnamon.
6. **Bake the schnecken:** Preheat oven to 350°F. and grease a standard muffin tin with butter or nonstick baking spray.

(Continued on next page)

7. Deflate the dough and transfer to a lightly floured surface. Roll out into a rectangle that's approximately 12 x 24 inches.
8. Spread the filling mixture over the dough in an even layer. Starting with one long side, roll the dough into a log. Cut the dough into twelve 2-inch slices.
9. Cover each generously with topping, being sure to adhere it to the sides as well as the top, and transfer to prepared muffin tin.
10. Loosely cover with a piece of lightly oiled plastic wrap or a damp kitchen towel and let rise about 10 minutes, until slightly puffed and rounded.
11. Bake 25 to 30 minutes, until browned. Let cool on the sheet 10 minutes and then transfer to a wire rack to cool completely.

Party Time:
Cakes and Cupcakes

Sour Cream Cheesecake

Makes one 9-inch cheesecake

Before I had the opportunity to run William Greenberg, I ran my own baking company called Bread and Batter—I was selling challah, but the very first dessert friends and customers started asking me for was cheesecake. I tried a handful of different recipes, mixing and matching until I found the combination of ingredients that made the type of cheesecake I like best: very smooth, very soft, and very creamy. I find that the key to its texture is to bake it in a water-bath (a.k.a. bain marie), which provides gentle, even heat.

Crust:

6 tablespoons butter, melted, divided

1 cup graham cracker crumbs

1 tablespoon sugar

Filling:

2½ pounds cream cheese, soft at room temperature

1½ cups sugar, divided

⅛ teaspoon kosher salt

⅓ cup sour cream

2 teaspoons vanilla extract

2 teaspoons lemon juice

6 eggs plus 2 yolks, at room temperature

1. Heat oven to 325°F. Grease a 9-inch springform pan with 1 tablespoon of melted butter. Wrap the bottom edge of the pan with aluminum foil to prevent leaks.
2. **Make the crust:** Combine graham cracker crumbs, sugar, and remaining 5 tablespoons of melted butter in a medium bowl until moist. Press crumbs onto bottom of pan, packing them firmly with the bottom of a measuring cup or glass. Bake for 10 minutes, until fragrant and firm, then let cool completely.
3. **Make the filling:** Use a stand mixer or handheld electric beaters to beat the cream cheese until very smooth. Add half of the sugar and beat until sugar has dissolved, about 2 minutes. Add remaining sugar, salt, sour cream, vanilla, and lemon juice and beat to combine. Add eggs and beat until mixture is smooth and homogenous.
4. When the crust is cool, place the springform pan in a large baking or roasting dish. Bring a kettle of water to a boil. Pour filling onto cooled crust, then carefully pour hot water from the kettle into your baking dish so that it reaches halfway up the sides of the springform pan. Carefully transfer to the oven and bake for 1 hour, until set on the edges but still wobbly in the center. Turn off oven, crack the door, and let cake cool for 30 minutes before removing.
5. Transfer pan to a rack. When completely cooled, cover with foil and refrigerate for at least 4 hours.

Do-ahead: *The cheesecake can be made 2 days in advance. Store in the refrigerator, covered with foil.*

Apple Macaroon Cake

Makes one 8-inch cake

We can't keep this cake on the shelf during Rosh Hashanah (or Passover, when we tweak the recipe to make it Pesach-friendly). Rich, dense, and almondy, with a layer of sweet apples crowning the top, it's a perfect fall dessert. You can arrange the apple slices haphazardly or, for a special occasion, take the time to arrange them in concentric circles. Do be sure to buy almond paste—marzipan is much sweeter and smoother than almond paste and won't produce the same effect.

- 1 pound (1¾ cups) almond paste, broken into chunks
- 1 cup sugar, divided
- ½ teaspoon kosher salt
- 6 egg yolks
- 1 cup egg whites (from about 8 eggs)
- ⅔ cup flour
- 3 Granny Smith apples, peeled and sliced into ⅓-inch wedges

1. Preheat oven to 325°F. Grease an 9-inch springform pan with butter, line the bottom with a circle of parchment paper, and butter the parchment.
2. In the bowl of a food processor, pulse almond paste, ½ cup of sugar, and salt until uniformly sandy, about 30 pulses.
3. Add the yolks and process until thick and smooth, about 30 seconds, scraping down the bowl halfway through.
4. In a medium separate bowl, whisk together egg whites and remaining ½ cup of sugar until incorporated but not peaked: The mixture should be fairly frothy but shouldn't hold any shape. Gently whisk in flour.
5. Add egg white mixture to the food processor and process for 10 seconds. Scrape down the bowl and process for about 5 seconds more until you have a smooth batter.
6. Pour batter into prepared pan and arrange apple slices on top.
7. Bake 60 to 70 minutes, until toothpick comes out clean. Run a knife around the side of the pan to loosen the cake, then cool in pan 10 minutes. Transfer to a wire rack to cool completely.

Do-ahead: *Cake can be made 5 days ahead. Cover with foil and store in the refrigerator.*

All Chocolate Cake

Makes one 9-inch cake

This cake might look demure, but don't be fooled: Its short stature and humble appearance belies its power. Dense, rich, and fudgy, this is a real chocolate lover's dream. I prefer to serve it at room temperature, when the cake and bittersweet ganache meld together, but I know some customers like to serve it cold, like a chilled chocolate bar.

Cake:

1¾ cups flour
½ cup unsweetened cocoa powder
1½ teaspoons baking powder
½ teaspoon baking soda
½ teaspoon kosher salt
1½ sticks butter
6 ounces bittersweet chocolate, chopped
3 eggs
½ cup milk
1¾ cups sugar
1½ teaspoons vanilla extract

Ganache:

1¼ cups heavy cream
2 tablespoons butter
12 ounces semisweet chocolate, chopped
½ teaspoon vanilla extract

1. **Make the cake:** Preheat oven to 325° and butter a high-sided 9-inch cake pan. Line the bottom with a circle of parchment paper, butter the parchment, and flour the pan.
2. In a medium bowl, whisk together flour, cocoa, baking powder, baking soda, and salt.
3. In a large saucepan over low heat, melt the chocolate and the butter, stirring until smooth. Let cool for 5 minutes, then whisk in eggs and milk until smooth. Add sugar and vanilla and whisk vigorously until the sugar is dissolved and the mixture is glossy and shiny.
4. Fold in the flour mixture just until no dry streaks remain, being careful not to overmix.
5. Pour into prepared cake pan.
6. Bake 60 to 75 minutes, until set with a firm crust, and a toothpick comes out clean.
7. Cool in pan on a rack for 15 minutes, then invert onto a rack to cool completely.
8. **Make the ganache:** In a small saucepan, combine the cream and butter and bring to a bare simmer. Place the chopped chocolate in a heatproof bowl.
9. Pour the hot cream mixture over the chocolate and let sit for 30 seconds. Add the vanilla and whisk until smooth. Cool, stirring occasionally, until thick, about 1 hour, and spread to cover the top and sides of the cake.

Do-ahead: *Cake can be made and frosted 1 to 2 days ahead. Cover with foil and keep at a cool room temperature.*

German Chocolate Cake

Makes one 8-inch layer cake

I'd always assumed that the German chocolate cake we've been selling at William Greenberg for as long as I can remember originated in Germany—but, as turns out, I'd been mistaken. This chocolate cake, with its signature coconut-pecan frosting, gets its name from Samuel German, a baker who developed a dark baking chocolate for Baker's Chocolate Company in 1852. And the chocolate only took off in 1957, when a reader-submitted recipe that called for the product appeared in the Dallas Morning News *and got picked up and distributed by General Foods, which owned the Baker's brand. Mr. Greenberg, who had already been in business for over a decade, must've caught wind of the cake's popularity and thought to serve his own version—chocolatey layer cakes sandwiched with chocolate fudge and covered in creamy coconut icing—at the bakery.*

Cake:

2½ cups flour
¼ cup unsweetened cocoa powder
¾ teaspoon baking powder
1 teaspoon baking soda
½ teaspoon kosher salt
5 ounces semisweet chocolate, chopped
½ cup coffee
3 sticks butter, softened
2 cups granulated sugar
2 eggs
1 teaspoon vanilla extract
1 cup buttermilk

Assembly:

1 cup chopped pecans, toasted

Coconut frosting:

1 cup evaporated milk
½ cup light brown sugar
½ cup granulated sugar
1 stick butter, cut into pieces
3 egg yolks
¼ teaspoon kosher salt
1 cup chopped pecans
1½ cups sweetened shredded coconut
2 teaspoons vanilla extract

Chocolate fudge frosting:

4 tablespoons butter
5 ounces Baker's Chocolate, chopped
1 cup confectioners' sugar
½ cup evaporated milk
½ teaspoon vanilla extract

(Continued on next page)

1. **Make the cakes:** Preheat oven to 350°F. Generously butter three 8-inch round cake pans and line the bottoms with parchment circles.
2. In a large bowl, whisk together the flour, cocoa powder, baking powder, baking soda, and salt.
3. In a double boiler or in a small bowl in the microwave working in 20-second increments, melt the chopped chocolate with the coffee. Stir until smooth.
4. In the bowl of a stand mixer fitted with the paddle attachment or working with electric beaters in a large bowl, beat the butter on medium-high speed until smooth. Add the granulated sugar and continue to beat until light and fluffy, about 3 to 4 minutes. Add the eggs and vanilla and continue to beat until fully incorporated, scraping down the sides of the bowl as needed. Beat in the melted chocolate. Reduce speed to low and beat in the dry ingredients in 3 additions, alternating with buttermilk in 2 additions, until you have a smooth batter.
5. Divide the batter into the three cake pans and bake for 25 to 35 minutes, until a toothpick comes out clean.
6. Allow cakes to cool for 10 minutes in the pans before turning out onto wire racks to cool completely.
7. **Make the coconut frosting:** In a medium saucepan, stir together the evaporated milk, brown sugar, granulated sugar, butter, egg yolks, and salt. Bring to a low boil over medium heat, stirring constantly until the sauce thickens and darkens to a pale caramel color, about 6 minutes. Remove from heat.
8. Stir in the pecans, coconut, and vanilla and let cool completely.
9. **Make the chocolate fudge frosting:** In a double boiler or in a small bowl in the microwave working in 20-second increments, melt the butter and chocolate. Stir until smooth. In a medium bowl, whisk together the confectioners' sugar, evaporated milk, and vanilla. Pour in the chocolate mixture and whisk until you have a spreadable consistency, about 30 seconds.
10. **To assemble:** Place one cake layer on a plate and spread with a thin layer of chocolate fudge frosting and one third of the coconut frosting. Repeat with the second and third layers.
11. Frost the sides with the remaining chocolate frosting, then arrange the chopped pecans all around the bottom half of the cake

Do-ahead: *Cakes and coconut frosting can be made 1 day ahead—wrap cakes in plastic and store at room temperature or in the fridge. Cover coconut frosting with plastic wrap and store in the fridge. Allow to come to room temperature before using.*

Red Velvet Cake with Cream Cheese Frosting

Makes one 8-inch layer cake

The popularity of our red velvet cake is undisputed year-round but reaches its peak at Valentine's Day. The genesis of red velvet can be traced to the early 1940s when a food dye business called Adams Extract Company souped up a devil's food-esque chocolate cake with tons of red coloring and began distributing the recipe as part of their marketing campaign. The cake enjoyed a second wind when it made a cameo in the movie Steel Magnolias. *It's great when you're craving a little bit of chocolate but not too much—and if I'm being honest, I make it as an excuse to eat lots of cream cheese frosting.*

Cake:

2 cups flour
¼ cup unsweetened cocoa powder
1 teaspoon baking powder
1 teaspoon baking soda
½ teaspoon kosher salt
2 cups sugar
1 cup canola oil
2 eggs
1¼ cups buttermilk
2 teaspoons vanilla extract
1 teaspoon white vinegar
1½ ounces red food coloring

Frosting:

1 stick butter, softened
8 ounces cream cheese, softened
1½ teaspoons vanilla extract
¼ teaspoon kosher salt
4 cups confectioners' sugar

1. **Make the cakes:** Preheat oven to 325°F. Butter and flour two 8-inch cake pans.
2. In a medium bowl, whisk together the flour, cocoa powder, baking powder, baking soda, and salt.
3. Working with a stand mixer fitted with a paddle attachment or working with electric beaters and a large bowl, beat the sugar and oil on medium speed until sugar is partially dissolved and mixture looks creamy, 3 to 4 minutes.
4. Mix in the eggs and buttermilk, beating to combine.
5. Add the vanilla, vinegar, and food coloring.
6. Reduce speed to low and gradually add the flour mixture and beat just until no dry streaks remain.
7. Divide between prepared cake pans.
8. Bake 45 to 50 minutes, until a toothpick comes out with moist crumbs.
9. Cool 20 minutes in the pans on a rack, then invert cakes onto a rack to cool completely.

(Continued on page 95)

10. **Make the frosting:** Working with a stand mixer fitted with a paddle attachment or working with electric beaters and a large bowl, beat the butter and the cream cheese on medium-high speed until fluffy, 4 to 5 minutes. Beat in the vanilla and salt. Reduce speed to low and gradually add the confectioners' sugar until well combined.
11. **Assemble the cake:** Using a sharp serrated knife, cut the cake layers in half so that you have four layers. Place one layer on a serving plate, then spread a layer of frosting on top. Repeat with two additional layers of cake (three total), then spread the remaining frosting over the top and sides of the cake. Break up the remaining fourth layer into small crumbs, then press gently to adhere the crumbs to the top and sides of the cake.

Do-ahead: *The frosted cake can be refrigerated for up to 2 days. The cake layers can be wrapped tightly in plastic wrap for up to 3 days before assembly.*

Cake Diane

Makes one 8-inch layer cake

For chocolate lovers only! This tower of cocoa-chocolate cake, chocolate mousse, and chocolate ganache is simply divine. Save it for the most decadent, romantic occasions like Valentine's Day, or a special anniversary celebration—or just a chilly afternoon when you're in the mood for a baking project. And if you want to skip the cake and the ganache and beeline straight for the mousse, be my guest. It's good enough to eat with a spoon—but a dollop of unsweetened whipped cream wouldn't hurt.

Cake:

1½ cups cake flour
¾ cup cocoa powder
1½ teaspoons baking soda
1 teaspoon baking powder
1 teaspoon kosher salt
1½ sticks butter, softened
1½ cups sugar
5 eggs
¾ cup milk
1 teaspoon vanilla extract

Mousse:

6 ounces semisweet chocolate, chopped
2 tablespoons cocoa powder
½ cup hot water
2 cups heavy cream
2 tablespoons sugar

Ganache:

1¼ cups heavy cream
2 tablespoons butter
12 ounces semisweet chocolate, chopped
¼ teaspoon vanilla extract

1. **Make the cakes:** Preheat the oven to 325°F. Generously butter three 8-inch cake pans, line with parchment circles, butter the parchment, and dust with flour, tapping to shake off any excess.
2. In a large bowl, whisk together the flour, cocoa, baking soda, baking powder, and salt.
3. In the bowl of a stand mixer fitted with a paddle attachment or working with electric beaters and a large bowl, cream together the butter and sugar on medium speed until light and fluffy, 4 to 5 minutes, scraping down the sides of the bowl occasionally.
4. In a separate bowl, whisk together the eggs, milk, and vanilla until frothy, 1 minute.
5. Gradually pour the egg mixture into the butter mixture and beat on medium-low speed until well combined; the mixture will appear curdled.
6. Reduce speed to low and gradually add the flour mixture, beating just until no dry streaks remain.
7. Divide the batter between the three prepared pans.
8. Bake 25 to 30 minutes, until a toothpick comes out clean.
9. Cool cakes in pans on wire racks for 10 minutes. Then invert onto racks to cool completely.

(Continued on next page)

10. **Make the mousse:** Melt chocolate in a double boiler or in a medium heatproof bowl in the microwave in 20-second increments. Combine the water and cocoa powder and add to the melted chocolate. Stir to combine and let cool.
11. In the bowl of a stand mixer fitted with a whisk attachment or working with electric beaters and a large bowl, beat the cream and sugar together until stiff peaks appear.
12. Fold in the cooled chocolate mixture.
13. Refrigerate until needed.
14. **Make the ganache:** In a small saucepan, combine the cream and butter and bring to a bare simmer. Place the chopped chocolate in a heatproof bowl.
15. Pour the hot cream over the chocolate and let sit for 30 seconds. Add the vanilla and whisk until smooth. Let cool until thick and spreadable.
16. **Assemble the cake:** Spread a layer of the mousse over one layer of cake. Top with another cake layer and repeat this process so that you have three layers of cake and two layers of mousse. Spread the cooled ganache of top and the sides of cake.

Do-ahead: *Cake can be assembled 3 days ahead. Covered with foil or plastic and keep refrigerated. Mousse and cake layers can be made 2 days ahead. Cover with plastic and refrigerate.*

Candy Cake

Makes one 8-inch layer cake

By far the bakery's most popular cake, this iconic creation is the cake for birthday parties and special occasions: One couple even asked us to turn it into their wedding cake! The flavor is more akin to Devil's Food than to Death by Chocolate—the richness comes from the whipped cream, shaved chocolate, and pure chocolate wafers rather than the cake itself.

We make the chocolate wafers in house, and I've included simple instructions so that you can, too. Of course, if you want to buy the chocolate wafers, that'll do the trick—just make sure they're light enough that they won't slip down the whipped cream-covered sides.

Cake:

1½ cups flour
¾ cup cocoa powder
2 teaspoons baking soda
1 teaspoon baking powder
1 teaspoon kosher salt
2 sticks butter, softened
1½ cups sugar
5 eggs
½ cup milk
½ teaspoon vanilla extract

Chocolate wafers:

8 ounces milk or dark chocolate, coarsely chopped

Assembly:

2 cups heavy cream, cold
¼ cup confectioners' sugar
½ teaspoon vanilla extract
Milk or dark chocolate, for decorating

1. **Make the cakes:** Preheat oven to 350°F. Generously butter two 8-inch cake pans, then line the bottoms with parchment paper circles.
2. In a medium bowl, whisk the flour, cocoa powder, baking powder, baking soda, and salt to combine. In the bowl of a stand mixer fitted with the paddle attachment or working with electric beaters in a large bowl, cream together the butter and sugar on medium-high speed until light and fluffy, 4 to 5 minutes.
3. In a small bowl or liquid measuring cup, whisk together eggs, milk, and vanilla. Add the egg mixture to the butter and beat on medium-low speed until well-combined, scraping down the sides of the bowl as necessary, 2 to 3 minutes; the mixture will appear curdled. Reduce speed to low and gradually add dry ingredients, mixing just until no dry streaks remain.
4. Divide batter evenly between the two prepared pans. Bake 30 to 35 minutes, rotating front to back and top to bottom halfway through, until a toothpick comes out clean.
5. Transfer the cakes to a rack, run an offset spatula or butter knife around the edges to release any sticking bits, and allow to cool completely in the pan before inverting.

(Continued on page 101)

6. **Make the chocolate wafers:** Line a baking sheet with parchment paper. Melt the chocolate in a double boiler or in a medium bowl in the microwave in 20-second increments until smooth. Remove from the heat and spread into a thin, even layer on prepared baking sheet. Put the baking sheet in the freezer and freeze until firm, about 10 minutes. If the chocolate is too brittle to cut without breaking, let sit at room temperature until just pliable. Transfer parchment sheet to a cutting board and cut chocolate into 1-inch square wafers. Refrigerate until ready to use.
7. **Assemble the cake:** Combine heavy cream, confectioners' sugar, and vanilla in the bowl of a stand mixer fitted with a whisk attachment or a large bowl. Whip until stiff peaks form.
8. Use a long serrated knife to cut each cake into two layers. Spread a layer of whipped cream between each and stack. Cover the top and outside with the whipped cream.
9. Use a microplane to grate chocolate all over the middle of the cake, then decorate the top edge with chocolate wafers.

Do ahead: *Cakes can be made 3 days in advance. Turn out of cake pans, wrap in plastic, and store in the fridge. Assembled cake can be made 1 day ahead. Tent with aluminum foil and store in the fridge.*

I Want Candy

When a customer walks into the bakery looking for a cake, chances are high that they'll walk out with the Candy Cake. Because it looks so impressive and pleases a crowd (who doesn't love the combination of chocolate and cream?), it's been the top-selling cake since Mr. Greenberg put it on the menu decades ago.

The Candy Cake's look is iconic: whipped cream that zig-zags down the sides of the cake (the piping is totally optional when you're making the cake at home), grated chocolate that covers the center, and thin chocolate wafers that form a banister around the perimeter. Mr. Greenberg created the cake in the 1940s, inspired by European cream cakes he admired during his wartime service.

Mr. Greenberg loved to decorate cakes. He used to come into the bakery each and every day, tie an apron over his polo shirt, and get to work on the special occasion cakes he made for generations of New Yorkers. Even though Mr. Greenberg is no longer decorating cakes, part of our consistency lies in the fact that we have the same main team of bakers who were trained by Mr. Greenberg himself, including our amazing cake decorator, Audrey. Audrey has been with us for more than two decades and makes Candy Cakes for weddings, bar and bat mitzvahs, and any kind of special occasion you can think of.

But lest we lose the institutional cake knowledge, we're training the next generation of bakers—the sons and daughters of the original crew—to take on more responsibility and absorb everything their parents learned from Mr. Greenberg. Long live the Candy Cake.

Do-ahead: *Cakes can be baked 3 days ahead. Wrap in plastic wrap and store in the refrigerator.*

Strawberry Cream Cake with Vanilla Frosting

Makes one 8-inch layer cake

Second in popularity only to the Candy Cake, this one is my personal favorite. Like the Candy Cake, it's soft and lush, with a fine, delicate crumb. As cakes come, it's on the fluffier side, not rich, dense, or buttery. I think the cake—simple and delicious—is the perfect backdrop for the purity of whipped cream and juicy red berries, a timeless combination. We sell this cake year-round, but of course it's best with high-summer's ripest, sweetest strawberries.

- 2 cups cake flour
- 1 cup all-purpose flour
- 1¼ teaspoons baking powder
- ½ teaspoon kosher salt
- 2 sticks butter, softened
- 1½ cups sugar
- 3 eggs
- 1 cup milk
- 1 teaspoon vanilla extract, divided
- 2 cups heavy cream, cold
- ½ cup confectioners' sugar
- 2 pounds strawberries, hulled, ⅓ very thinly sliced (about 1½ cups) and the rest left whole, for assembling

1. Heat oven to 350°F. Grease three 8-inch cake pans with butter or nonstick cooking spray, then line the bottoms with parchment paper circles.
2. In a medium bowl, sift together the flours, baking powder, and salt. In the bowl of a stand mixer or working with electric beaters in a large bowl, cream together the butter and sugar on medium-high speed until light and fluffy, 4 to 5 minutes, scraping down the bowl occasionally. In a small bowl, whisk together the eggs, milk, and ½ teaspoon vanilla. Add dry ingredients to the sugar-butter mixture in thirds, alternating with egg-milk mixture in two additions, until you have a smooth batter.
3. Divide evenly between prepared cake pans and bake for 25 to 30 minutes, until a toothpick comes out clean.
4. Transfer the cakes to a rack, run an offset spatula or butter knife around the edges to release any sticking bits, and allow to cool completely in the pan. Once cooled, use a serrated knife to carefully slice the domed portion off each cake, leveling the top surface.
5. When you're ready to assemble the cake, combine heavy cream, remaining ½ teaspoon vanilla, and confectioners' sugar in the bowl of a stand mixer fitted with a whisk attachment or a large bowl. Whip until stiff peaks form.
6. To assemble cake, spread a layer of cream on top of one cake. Add half of the sliced strawberries in an even layer over the cream. Cover with second cake layer and repeat the layer of whipped cream and strawberries. Top with the final layer, then spread remaining whipped cream over the entire cake and decorate the top with the whole strawberries.

Caramel Cake

Makes one 9-inch layer cake

You don't often see this southern-style cake in New York City, which explains why it's such a topic of conversation in the store: It seems like every day customers come in and are intrigued by the caramel-covered, almond-shellacked layer cake. The icing isn't a true caramel—it's a butterscotch sauce made of light brown sugar, butter, and evaporated milk—which means there's no risk of burning sugar. The toasty almonds, crunchy and nutty, are the perfect balance to the rich sweetness.

Cake:

1½ sticks butter, softened
1 cup milk
2 cups flour
2½ teaspoons baking powder
¼ teaspoon salt
4 eggs
1½ cups sugar
1½ teaspoons vanilla extract

Almond caramel:

½ cup slivered almonds
2¼ cups light brown sugar
1½ sticks butter, divided
½ cup evaporated milk
1 teaspoon vanilla
½ teaspoon kosher salt

1. **Make the cakes:** Preheat oven to 350°F. Butter and flour three 9-inch cake pans and line the bottoms with parchment paper rounds.
2. In a small saucepan over a low heat, heat the butter and milk until the butter melts. Stir well and let cool.
3. In a medium bowl, whisk together the flour, baking powder, and salt.
4. In the bowl of a stand mixer fitted with a paddle attachment or working with electric beaters and a large bowl, beat the eggs and sugar on medium speed until the sugar is dissolved and the mixture is well combined, 2 to 3 minutes.
5. Reduce the speed to low, add the flour mixture, and beat to combine.
6. Pour in the milk mixture and the vanilla and beat until smooth, scraping down the sides of the bowl as necessary.
7. Divide the batter between the three pans.
8. Bake 25 to 30 minutes, rotating top to bottom and front to back halfway through, or until a toothpick comes out clean.
9. Cool cakes completely in pans, then turn out and remove parchment. Slice the domed tops off the cakes to create even layers.
10. Lower oven to 250°F.

(Continued on next page)

11. Spread the slivered almonds on a baking sheet and bake for 5 minutes, until very lightly toasted.
12. **Make the frosting:** In a medium saucepan, combine the light brown sugar, 8 tablespoons of butter, and evaporated milk and bring to a boil over medium heat. Whisk well and lower heat to simmer. Cook for about 10 minutes without stirring until it darkens slightly and thickens considerably. Remove from heat and add vanilla, salt, and the remaining 4 tablespoons of butter, whisking until the butter melts completely. Transfer to a heatproof bowl, add the toasted almonds, and stir to coat. Let cool for about 25 minutes, stirring occasionally, until thick but still pourable.
13. Working quickly, as the mixture will set rapidly, spread a thin layer of icing over the top of one layer, place second layer on top, then repeat with another layer of frosting and the third layer. Ice the top and sides with remaining caramel.

Do-ahead: *Cake layers can be made 3 days ahead. Wrap in plastic and store in the refrigerator. Assembled cake can be made 2 days ahead. Cover loosely with foil and store in the refrigerator.*

Lemon Meringue Cake

Makes one 9-inch layer cake

Lemon desserts are my favorite and this one is possibly the best. Our customers think so, too. We keep this cake in the case year-round and it goes fast every day. It has all the pleasure of lemon meringue pie with rich tangy curd and toasted meringue, plus the comfort of tender cake. It's a great showstopper dessert for any celebration. You can even double the amounts below for an extra impressive tower.

Lemon curd:

3 eggs
¾ cup sugar
¾ cup fresh lemon juice
⅛ teaspoon kosher salt
1 stick butter, softened, cut into pieces

Cake:

Butter and flour, for the pans
3 cups cake flour
1 tablespoon baking powder
½ teaspoon kosher salt
2 sticks butter, softened
2 cups sugar
4 large eggs
4 large egg yolks
1 teaspoon vanilla extract
1 cup whole milk

Meringue frosting:

1¾ cups sugar
¾ teaspoon fresh lemon juice
1 cup egg whites (from about 8 eggs)

1. **Make the curd:** In a double boiler or a medium heatproof bowl set over a pot of simmering water, combine the eggs, sugar, lemon juice, and salt. Whisk constantly until the mixture becomes thick and opaque, about 10 minutes. Add the butter and remove from heat.
2. Vigorously stir until the butter has melted and the mixture is smooth and glossy.
3. Transfer to a bowl and cool slightly. Place a piece of plastic directly on the curd and refrigerate until well-chilled, at least 4 hours.
4. **Make the cakes:** Preheat the oven to 350°F. Butter three 9-inch-round cake pans, line the bottoms with parchment, and butter the parchment. Dust the pans with flour, tapping out excess.
5. Into a large bowl, sift the flour, baking powder, and salt. In the bowl of a stand mixer fitted with the paddle attachment, beat the butter and sugar on medium-high speed until fluffy, 4 to 5 minutes, scraping down the sides of the bowl occasionally. Reduce the speed to medium and beat in the eggs and egg yolks, one at a time. Beat in the vanilla. Scrape the bowl. Turn the speed to low and add the flour mixture in thirds, alternating with the milk in two additions. Beat just until smooth. Divide the batter between the three prepared pans, smoothing the tops.

(Continued on page 111)

6. Bake until a toothpick inserted in the centers comes out clean, about 25 to 30 minutes.
7. Cool in the pans on a wire rack for 10 minutes, then unmold and discard the parchment. Cool completely on the rack.
8. **Make the frosting:** Bring a saucepan of water to a simmer. In the bowl of a stand mixer, whisk the sugar, lemon juice, and egg whites. Set the bowl over the simmering water and whisk until the sugar dissolves and the mixture is very warm to the touch. When you rub some between your fingers, you shouldn't feel any grains of sugar. Fit the bowl into the mixer with the whisk attachment and beat on medium speed until the meringue is cool, fluffy, thick, and shiny, about 10 minutes. Stiff peaks should form when you lift the whisk from the bowl. To assemble the cake, put one layer, cut side up, on a heatproof cake plate. Spread half of the curd evenly over the cake and top with another layer, cut side up. Repeat the layering, putting the cut side down on the top layer.
9. Spread the meringue frosting over the sides and top of the cake, swirling peaks all around. Use a kitchen torch to toast the meringue dark golden brown.

Do-ahead: *The frosted cake should be served the day it's made, but the cake layers can be wrapped tightly in plastic wrap for up to 3 days before assembly. The cake layers stacked with the curd can be wrapped tightly and refrigerated for up to 1 day. The curd itself can be made 1 week in advance and stored in the fridge.*

Do-ahead: *Unglazed cake can be made 1 week ahead. Wrap in plastic and store at room temperature.*

Orange-Glazed Angel Food Cake

Makes one 8-inch cake

I'll admit it: No one considers angel food cake—with its cloud-white fluff devoid of butter, egg yolks, or any fun add-ins like chocolate chips or nuts—to be the most exciting cake in the books. Which is why we spiff ours up with a citrus glaze that slides down the sides and offers each slice a glossy finish.

A tip about slicing: Angel food cake is bouncy, which means it's resistant to knives. To slice neatly without squishing or smashing, use your sharpest chef's knife or serrated knife and make gentle sawing motions, moving away from you and toward you rather than pressing down into the cake.

Cake:

1 cup cake flour
1½ cups sugar, divided
1¼ cups egg whites (from about 10 eggs)
1½ teaspoons cream of tartar
¼ teaspoon kosher salt
1 teaspoon vanilla extract
¼ teaspoon almond extract

Glaze:

1½ cups confectioners' sugar, plus more as needed
¼ cup orange juice, plus more as needed
1 tablespoon orange zest
Orange food coloring, optional

1. **Make the cake:** Preheat oven to 325°F.
2. Sift together the flour and ¾ cup of sugar into a medium bowl two times.
3. In the bowl of a stand mixer fitted with the whisk attachment, beat the egg whites on medium-low speed until foamy, 1 minute 30 seconds.
4. Add the cream of tartar and salt, gradually increase the speed to medium-high, and continue to beat until soft peaks form, another 1 minute 30 seconds.
5. Add the remaining ¾ cup sugar and continue whipping until the meringue is glossy and white and thick enough that it holds stiff peaks, 1 minute. Add the vanilla and almond extracts and beat to combine.
6. Sift a third of the flour mixture over the eggs and use a rubber spatula to fold until no flour is visible. Repeat with two more flour additions.
7. Pour into an 8-inch angel food cake pan with a removable bottom and bake for 1 hour, or until it's golden and springs back to touch.
8. Invert pan and cool on a rack upside down until no warmth remains, at least 2 hours. Slide an offset spatula or butter knife around the sides of the cake to loosen, then remove from pan and invert onto a serving platter.
9. **Make the glaze:** Mix the confectioners' sugar with the orange juice. If your glaze is too thin or thick, add more confectioners' sugar or juice, respectively, until you have a thick but pourable consistency. Optionally add a couple drops of orange food coloring. Whisk in orange zest. Pour over cooled cake.

Espresso Cake with Mocha Buttercream

Makes one 8-inch layer cake

While we're known as a kosher bakery, we celebrate and revere all holidays and are especially busy around Christmas time. This cake had its origins as a bûche de noël and quickly became a favorite. The assembly was simplified into a layer cake that is a year-round staple.

Cake:

6 large eggs, separated, room temperature
1 cup sugar
1 tablespoon instant coffee
¼ teaspoon kosher salt
1 cup flour
1 teaspoon baking powder

Mocha buttercream:

2 sticks unsalted butter, room temperature
1 ounce unsweetened chocolate, melted and cooled
1 large egg yolk, beaten
2½ cups confectioners' sugar, sifted
1 teaspoon instant coffee
1 teaspoon pure vanilla extract
¼ teaspoon kosher salt

1. **Make the cakes:** Preheat the oven to 350°F. Line the bottoms of three 8-inch-round cake pans with parchment paper.
2. Working with a stand mixer fitted with a paddle attachment or working with electric beaters and a large bowl, beat the egg yolks on medium-high speed until thick and lemon-colored, about 1 minute. Add the sugar, coffee, and salt and beat until ribbons of batter sit on the surface when you lift the beaters or paddle, about 4 minutes. In another bowl, whisk the egg whites with an electric mixer or by hand until stiff but not dry peaks form, about 3 minutes.
3. Sift the flour and baking powder directly over the yolk mixture. Gently fold until no traces of flour remain. Add one third of the egg whites and stir until incorporated and the mixture has lightened. Add the remaining whites and fold gently until incorporated and no streaks remain. Divide the batter between the three prepared pans, smoothing the tops.
4. Bake until the tops spring back a bit when pressed gently, 25 to 30 minutes. Cool in the pans on a wire rack for 10 minutes. Run a sharp, thin knife around the edges of the cakes. Unmold, discard the parchment, and cool completely on the rack.
5. **Make the buttercream:** Working in a stand mixer fitted with the paddle attachment or working with electric mixers and

(Continued on next page)

a large bowl, beat the butter in the bowl until smooth and creamy. Add the chocolate, egg yolk, confectioners' sugar, coffee, vanilla, and salt. Beat on low speed until smooth, then raise the speed to medium and beat until fluffy.

6. **Assemble the cake:** Put one cake on a cake plate, smooth side up. Spread a generous amount of the buttercream on top. Center a second cake over top on top, smooth side up, spread over more frosting, and top with the final layer. Spread the remaining buttercream all over the sides and top.

Do-ahead: *The frosted cake can be refrigerated for up to 2 days. The cake layers can be wrapped tightly in plastic wrap for up to 3 days before assembly.*

Coconut Cream Cake with Shredded Coconut Buttercream

Makes one 9-inch layer cake

While this cake is one of our big sellers all year round, it's most popular during the spring, and especially around Easter and Mother's Day. Something about its all-white appearance feels refreshing and new—like that first breezy bright day after the cold, gray winter. There are a couple of ingredients that make this coconut cake special: First, the almond extract, which brings out the coconut's . . . well, nuttiness. The flavor of the cake would be a lot flatter without it. Second, the buttermilk: Its acidity reins in some of the cake's sweetness and helps to keep the crumb light and tender. Third, the cream cheese in the frosting, which adds the addictive tang that makes the icing on carrot cake so irresistible. And lastly, the coconut extract, which has a concentrated flavor that can't be replicated or matched. It's worth seeking out: Order a couple of bottles online and keep them in the pantry so that you're always ready to bake this stunning dessert.

Cake:

2½ cups cake flour
1 tablespoon baking powder
½ teaspoon salt
1½ sticks butter, softened
1½ cups sugar
2 eggs
1 teaspoon vanilla extract
½ teaspoon almond extract
1 teaspoon coconut extract
¾ cup buttermilk

Frosting:

1 stick butter, softened
12 ounces cream cheese, softened
5 cups confectioners' sugar
3 tablespoons heavy cream
½ teaspoon coconut extract
¼ teaspoon kosher salt
2 cups sweetened shredded coconut, divided

1. **Make the cakes:** Preheat oven to 350°F. Generously butter three 9-inch cake pans and line bottoms with parchment paper circles.
2. In a medium bowl, whisk together the flour, baking powder, and salt.
3. In the bowl of a stand mixer fitted with the paddle attachment or working with electric beaters in a large bowl, cream together the butter and sugar on medium-high speed until light and

(Continued on page 119)

fluffy, 4 to 5 minutes, scraping the bowl occasionally. Add the eggs one at a time, beating to incorporate after each addition. Add the vanilla, almond, and coconut extracts. Reduce speed to low and add the buttermilk, scraping down the sides of the bowl as needed, until you have a smooth batter. Gradually add the flour mixture, beating just until no dry streaks remain.

4. Divide batter evenly between the three prepared cake pans and bake 25 to 30 minutes, until a toothpick comes out clean.
5. Let cakes cool 10 minutes in pans before inverting onto wire racks to cool completely.
6. **Make the frosting:** Beat the butter and cream cheese together until combined. Add the confectioners' sugar, cream, coconut extract, and salt, and beat until light and fluffy, about 2 minutes. Fold in 1 cup of the shredded coconut.
7. **Assemble the cake:** Place one layer on a plate or cake stand. Spread a layer of frosting and top with second layer. Repeat with more frosting and the final layer. Spread the remaining frosting on the top and sides. Gently press the remaining 1 cup coconut to the top and sides of the cake.

Do-ahead: *Cakes can be made 3 days ahead. Wrap tightly in plastic and store in the fridge. Frosting, without the addition of coconut, can be made 3 days ahead and stored in the fridge. Before using allow to come to room temperature, beat well to loosen, and stir in the coconut.*

"Seven" Layer Cake

Makes one 8-by-4-inch layer cake

There's no way around it—this recipe, which comes from William Greenberg himself—is a lot of work! But it is a constant bestseller at the bakery, especially during the holidays, when we seem to be selling slices and entire cakes constantly—and for good reason. There are few cakes as decadent or celebratory as this striped stunner, the ancestor of which is the Hungarian dobos torte. It consists of nearly as much coffee-cocoa filling as it does cake—a winning ratio, if you ask me. A small secret: Our seven-layer cake is actually composed of just six (hence the quotes). We figure that once you get above five, no one's going to notice if a layer or two is missing, right?

Cake:

1½ cups flour
1 teaspoon baking powder
½ teaspoon kosher salt
2 sticks butter, softened
¾ cup sugar
4 eggs
1½ teaspoons vanilla extract

Filling:

2 sticks butter, softened
2¼ cups confectioners' sugar
¼ cup heavy cream
⅓ cup unsweetened cocoa powder
1 teaspoon instant coffee granules
¼ teaspoon kosher salt

Glaze:

4 tablespoons butter, melted
5 tablespoons cocoa powder
¼ cup hot water
1¾ cups confectioners' sugar
1½ teaspoons vanilla extract

1. **Make the cakes:** Preheat the oven to 350°F. Generously butter six 8x4-inch loaf pans (disposable aluminum pans work well here; if you don't have six, you'll need to work in batches).
2. In a small bowl, whisk together flour, baking powder, and salt.
3. In the bowl of a stand mixer fitted with a paddle attachment or working with electric beaters and a large bowl, cream the butter and sugar on medium-high until light and fluffy, 4 to 5 minutes. Beat in the eggs one at a time and add the vanilla, scraping down the sides of the bowl occasionally, until the batter is smooth and well-combined.
4. Reduce speed to low and gradually add the flour mixture, beating just until no dry streaks remain and scraping down the bowl two or three times.
5. Divide the batter evenly among the 6 pans. (For the most even layers, you'll want to weigh the batter, then divide it by 6 so that you know exactly how much to pour into each pan.)

(Continued on next page)

6. Bake for 12 to 15 minutes, until golden. Let cool 5 minutes in the pan before inverting onto a rack to cool completely. If using the same pan again, run under cold water until it's cool, dry well, and re-butter it.
7. **Make the filling:** In the bowl of a stand mixer fitted with a paddle attachment or working with electric beaters and a large bowl, beat the butter and confectioners' sugar on medium-high until light and fluffy, 4 to 5 minutes. Gradually add the cream and beat until combined. Beat in the cocoa, coffee, and salt and mix until smooth and thick.
8. **Make the glaze:** In a medium bowl, whisk together the butter, cocoa, and hot water. Mix in the sugar and vanilla, adding more hot water by the teaspoon if consistency is too thick. It should be pourable but not runny.
9. **Assemble the cake:** Spread a thin layer of filling on a cake layer. Place another cake on top and continue layering filling and cake until all layers are used. Pour glaze over the cake and, using a spatula, spread around the sides. Refrigerate for 1 hour, until firm enough to slice.

Do-ahead: *Layers can be made 3 days ahead. Wrap individually in plastic wrap and refrigerate. Assembled cake can be made 5 days ahead. Cover loosely and refrigerate.*

Rainbow Cake

Makes one 9-inch layer cake

For bakeries that have been around for generations, it's important to listen to the next generation to stay relevant. That's how this cake came to be one of our new bestsellers. My daughter saw a six-tiered rainbow cake while we were traveling and asked me to start making it. It's been flying out of our cases ever since. It is so eye-catching and beautiful that it makes eating it—and baking it—really fun. It's a bit labor intensive to make and frost six layers but well worth the effort. This cake has gotten a whole generation of kids excited about what we're doing at the bakery and may just have the same effect in your home kitchen, too.

Cake:

3 cups flour
1 tablespoon baking powder
½ teaspoon kosher salt
2 sticks butter, softened
2½ cups sugar
3 large eggs, room temperature
1 cup buttermilk
¼ cup heavy cream
1 tablespoon vanilla extract
Gel paste food coloring in red, yellow, blue, green, orange, and purple

Frosting:

12 ounces cream cheese, softened
3 sticks unsalted butter, softened
6 cups confectioners' sugar
1 tablespoon pure vanilla extract
¼ teaspoon kosher salt

1. **Make the cakes:** Position racks in the center, top and bottom of the oven, then preheat the oven to 350°F. Butter six 9-inch-round cake pans, line the bottoms with parchment, and butter the parchment. Dust the pans with flour, tapping out excess. If you don't have six pans, you can bake the batter in batches. Wash, dry, and prepare the pans as above after each batch. Keep the batter refrigerated until ready to bake.
2. In a large bowl, whisk together the flour, baking powder, and salt. In the bowl of a stand mixer fitted with the paddle attachment, beat the butter and sugar on medium-high speed until fluffy, 4 to 5 minutes, scraping down the sides of the bowl occasionally. Reduce the speed to medium and beat in the eggs, one at a time. Beat in the buttermilk, cream, and vanilla until well-blended; the mixture will appear curdled. Scrape the bowl. Turn the speed to low and gradually add half of the flour mixture. Scrape the bowl and then add the remaining flour, beating just until smooth.
3. Divide the batter evenly among six bowls. Add a few drops of each of the gel paste food colorings to the bowls, keeping the colors separate. Stir well and add more if you'd like deeper hues. Scrape the batters into the prepared pans, smoothing the tops.

(Continued on page 125)

4. Bake two pans on each rack, or in batches if needed, until a toothpick inserted in the centers comes out clean, 15 to 20 minutes.
5. Cool in the pans on a wire rack for 10 minutes, then unmold and discard the parchment. Cool completely on the rack.
6. **Make the frosting:** In the bowl of a stand mixer fitted with the paddle attachment, beat the cream cheese and butter on medium-high speed until smooth and creamy, scraping the bowl occasionally. Add the confectioners' sugar, vanilla, and salt and beat on low until blended. Scrape the bowl and beat on medium until fluffy.
7. **Assemble the cake:** Spread a scant ½ inch frosting between each cake layer, stacking them in any order you prefer. Spread the remaining frosting all over the sides and top of the cake.

Do-ahead: *The frosted cake can be refrigerated for up to 2 days. The cake layers can be wrapped tightly in plastic wrap for up to 3 days before assembly.*

Vanilla Cupcakes

Makes 2 dozen

Everyone needs a basic—but very good—vanilla cupcake recipe up their sleeve for bake sales, birthday parties, bridal showers, long weekends, or rainy afternoons. This is ours. Light and tender, they're topped with a simple-as-can-be American-style buttercream (that is, butter plus confectioners' sugar) that you can make a couple of days in advance. For kids' parties, I like to make the cupcakes and a big batch of uncolored frosting ahead of time, then let each child choose their color, decorate a couple cupcakes, and top them with as many sprinkles as they'd like.

Cupcakes:

1½ cups cake flour
1½ cups all-purpose flour
1½ teaspoons baking powder
¾ teaspoon salt
4 eggs
1 cup milk
1 teaspoon vanilla extract
2 sticks butter, softened
1¾ cups sugar

Buttercream:

2 sticks butter, softened
3 cups confectioners' sugar
3 tablespoons heavy cream
1½ teaspoons vanilla extract
¼ teaspoon salt
Food coloring

1. **Make the cupcakes:** Preheat oven to 350°F. Line two standard muffin tins with liners.
2. In a small bowl, whisk together the flours, baking powder, and salt. In a liquid measuring cup, whisk together the eggs, milk, and vanilla.
3. In the bowl of a stand mixer fitted with a paddle attachment or working with electric beaters and a large bowl, cream the butter and sugar on medium speed until light and fluffy, 4 to 5 minutes, scraping down the sides of the bowl occasionally. Add the flour mixture in thirds, alternating with the milk mixture in two additions, until you have a smooth batter.
4. Divide batter evenly among prepared pans, filling each cavity three-quarters full, and bake for 20 to 25 minutes, rotating front to back and top to bottom halfway through, until a toothpick comes out dry. Cool pan completely on wire rack before removing cupcakes.
5. **Make the frosting:** In a stand mixer fitted with a paddle attachment or working with electric beaters and a large bowl, beat the butter on medium-high speed until very light and fluffy, 2 to 3 minutes. Reduce speed to low and add confectioners' sugar gradually until incorporated, about 2 minutes. Add cream, vanilla, and salt and continue to mix. If needed, add more cream by the teaspoon to reach desired consistency. Add food coloring of choice (start with a little—you can always add more!) and beat to incorporate. Top each cupcake with frosting using a spoon, offset spatula, or butter knife.

Do-ahead: *Unfrosted cupcakes can be made 2 days ahead. Store in an airtight container. Buttercream can be made 2 days ahead. Store covered, with a layer of plastic wrap touching the surface, in the refrigerator. Bring to room temperature and beat until creamy before using.*

Chocolate Cupcakes

Makes 2 dozen

This is a simple variation on our vanilla cupcakes for chocolate fiends, with cocoa powder replacing some of the flour. We sell dozens of these tender cupcakes to children bringing them to school parties, adults hosting dinners and casual get-togethers, or customers who just need a dose of chocolate to get through the day. I especially love making cupcakes at home because they're simple to put together, they bake more quickly than whole cakes, and they're easier to decorate, with no slicing or stacking required.

Cupcakes:

2 cups cake flour
¾ cup cocoa powder
1½ teaspoons baking powder
1½ teaspoons baking soda
1 teaspoon kosher salt
4 eggs
1 cup milk
½ teaspoon vanilla extract
2 sticks butter, softened
1¾ cups sugar

Chocolate buttercream:

3 sticks butter, softened
¾ cups unsweetened cocoa powder
3 cups confectioners' sugar
¼ cup heavy cream, plus more as needed
1 tablespoon vanilla extract

1. **Make the cupcakes:** Preheat oven to 350°F. Line two standard muffin tins with liners.
2. In a small bowl, whisk together the flour, cocoa powder, baking powder, baking soda, and salt. In a liquid measuring cup, whisk together the eggs, milk, and vanilla.
3. In the bowl of a stand mixer fitted with a paddle attachment or working with electric beaters and a large bowl, cream the butter and sugar on medium speed until light and fluffy, 4 to 5 minutes. Add the flour mixture in thirds, alternating with the milk mixture in two additions, until you have a smooth batter.
4. Divide batter evenly among prepared pans, filling each cavity three-quarters full, and bake for 15-18 minutes, rotating front to back and top to bottom halfway through, until a toothpick comes out dry. Cool pan completely on wire rack before removing cupcakes.
5. **Make the buttercream:** In the bowl of a stand mixer fitted with a paddle attachment or working with electric beaters and a large bowl, cream the butter with the cocoa powder until smooth and well combined. Add sugar and cream in alternating additions, scraping down the sides of the bowl as necessary. If the frosting is too dry or pasty, add more cream by the tablespoon until you reach a smooth, spreadable consistency. Add vanilla and beat to combine. Top each cupcake with frosting using a spoon, offset spatula, or butter knife.

Acknowledgments

This book has been a dream of mine and a true labor of love. But it couldn't have been done without the love and labor of some very extraordinary people, too.

I want to thank Emily Becker, Zoe Cosgrove, Jodie Elyachar, Karen Kastenbaum, Wendy Krivit, Jeremy Moskowitz, and Betsy Scherl, all talented bakers, for their honest and serious feedback.

This project would never have happened without the energy, dedication, and hard work of Betsy Fox, Karen Gantz, Robin Insley, Sarah Jampel, Maggie Margolis, Laura Togut, and Leah Zarra.

Thank you all from the bottom of my heart.

Index

Conversion Charts

Metric and Imperial Conversions

(These conversions are rounded for convenience)

Ingredient	Cups/Tablespoons/ Teaspoons	Ounces	Grams/Milliliters
Butter	1 cup/ 16 tablespoons/ 2 sticks	8 ounces	230 grams
Cheese, shredded	1 cup	4 ounces	110 grams
Cream cheese	1 tablespoon	0.5 ounce	14.5 grams
Cornstarch	1 tablespoon	0.3 ounce	8 grams
Flour, all-purpose	1 cup/1 tablespoon	4.5 ounces/0.3 ounce	125 grams/8 grams
Flour, whole wheat	1 cup	4 ounces	120 grams
Fruit, dried	1 cup	4 ounces	120 grams
Fruits or veggies, chopped	1 cup	5 to 7 ounces	145 to 200 grams
Fruits or veggies, pureed	1 cup	8.5 ounces	245 grams
Honey, maple syrup, or corn syrup	1 tablespoon	0.75 ounce	20 grams
Liquids: cream, milk, water, or juice	1 cup	8 fluid ounces	240 milliliters
Oats	1 cup	5.5 ounces	150 grams
Salt	1 teaspoon	0.2 ounce	6 grams
Spices: cinnamon, cloves, ginger, or nutmeg (ground)	1 teaspoon	0.2 ounce	5 milliliters
Sugar, brown, firmly packed	1 cup	7 ounces	200 grams
Sugar, white	1 cup/1 tablespoon	7 ounces/0.5 ounce	200 grams/12.5 grams
Vanilla extract	1 teaspoon	0.2 ounce	4 grams

Oven Temperatures

Fahrenheit	Celsius	Gas Mark
225°	110°	¼
250°	120°	½
275°	140°	1
300°	150°	2
325°	160°	3
350°	180°	4
375°	190°	5
400°	200°	6
425°	220°	7
450°	230°	8